THE ATONEMENT IN MODERN RELIGIOUS THOUGHT.

THE ATONEMENT

IN MODERN RELIGIOUS THOUGHT.

A THEOLOGICAL SYMPOSIUM.

FRÉDERIC GODET.
ADOLF HARNACK.
AUGUSTE SABATIER.

LYMAN ABBOTT.
WASHINGTON GLADDEN.
T. T. MUNGER.

F. W. FARRAR.
W. H. FREMANTLE.

W. F. ADENEY.
R. J. CAMPBELL.
A. CAVE.
MARCUS DODS.
P. T. FORSYTH.
SILVESTER HORNE.
R. F. HORTON.
JOHN HUNTER.
BERNARD J. SNELL.

Second Edition.

WIPF & STOCK · Eugene, Oregon

Wipf and Stock Publishers
199 W 8th Ave, Suite 3
Eugene, OR 97401

The Atonement in Modern Religious Thought
A Theological Symposium
By Campbell, R. J.
ISBN 13: 978-1-5326-1084-4
Publication date 10/3/2016
Previously published by Mes Clarke & Co., 1902

PUBLISHERS' NOTE.

THE present volume consists of a series of articles on the Atonement contributed to *The Christian World* newspaper during the winter of 1899-1900. It may be taken as an answer to the question whether the Christian consciousness of to-day, in the view of modern historical, critical and ethical investigation, has any fresh affirmation to make, or any new attitude to assume, on this central doctrine of the Church's faith. The response comes, as will be seen, from distinguished representatives, not only of different ecclesiastical communions and of different nationalities, but of widely separated schools of religious thought. It would be a task of much interest to classify the different utterances, to exhibit their differences, and to endeavour to discover if such a residuum of harmony remains as might be taken to constitute the Church's common message on this theme. This, however, is obviously not the place for any such attempt. The articles are presented in the order in which they originally appeared. They are, it will be readily seen, intended as a discussion, and not as a theological ultimatum. Their object is not to dictate to, but to educate public opinion. They will have served their whole purpose in putting the reader in possession of the main considerations and lines of argument on which to construct a well-informed individual judgment on the great subject discussed.

CONTRIBUTORS.

FRÉDERIC GODET, D.D., *Neuchâtel, Switzerland.*
ADOLF HARNACK, D.D., *Professor of Church History in the University of Berlin.*
AUGUSTE SABATIER, *Dean of the Faculty of Protestant Theology of the University of Paris.*

LYMAN ABBOTT, D.D., *New York.*
WASHINGTON GLADDEN, D.D., *Columbus.*
T. T. MUNGER, D.D., *New Haven.*

F. W. FARRAR, D.D., *Dean of Canterbury.*
W. H. FREMANTLE, D.D., *Dean of Ripon.*

WALTER F. ADENEY, M.A., *Professor of New Testament Exegesis, History and Criticism, New College, London.*
R. J. CAMPBELL, B.A., *Brighton.*
ALFRED CAVE, B.A., D.D., *Principal of Hackney College.*
MARCUS DODS, D.D., *Professor of New Testament Exegesis in New College, Edinburgh.*
P. T. FORSYTH, M.A., D.D., *Cambridge.*
C. SILVESTER HORNE, M.A., *Kensington.*
R. F. HORTON, M.A., D.D., *formerly Fellow of New College, Oxford.*
JOHN HUNTER, D.D., *Glasgow.*
BERNARD J. SNELL, M.A., B.Sc., *Brixton.*

I.

BY R. J. CAMPBELL, B.A.
Brighton.

I.—PERSISTENCE OF THE DOCTRINE.

CHRIST is our Saviour from everything that humanity has cause to fear, and our Saviour to everything for which humanity ought to hope. The work of Christ in relation to human ill is redemption. Redemption has a general as well as a particular meaning. In its particular meaning it may be held to comprise the work of Christ in relation to *sin ;* in its generic sense it includes the work of Christ in relation to cosmical evil, that is, the putting right of everything that afflicts creation and man. The work of Christ in relation to sin is exhibited in the Christian doctrine of Atonement. We are all familiar with certain ideas included in it, ideas expressed by the words expiation, reconciliation, propitiation, ransom, satisfaction. Each of these aspects contains a certain truth, and the one doctrine which is held to include them all is the doctrine of Atonement.

If we could regard the doctrine of Atonement as a term of convenience to include the cognate ideas just stated, we could understand the significant place it has occupied in Christian history. The word atonement can hardly be called Scriptural, but the ideas which form its constituents are present or suggested on every page of the New Testament. No one will deny that the doctrine of Atonement has always been associated in a special way with the sufferings and death of Christ. In every one of the Christian centuries Christians, in speaking about their Master, have held that by His sufferings and death in some mysterious way a remedy has been provided for human sin. This statement may be challenged, but surely it is sufficiently true to be apparent to every one. We note from it that though theories of the Atonement have come and gone, belief in the fact has persisted and continues to persist. But any idea which persists for a long period of time in human history must be said to have value in human experience, and must somewhere or other contain a truth which answers to human need. Before we try to show what it is that in the doctrine of Atonement has persisted throughout the Christian centuries, it may be worth our while to look at some of the ways in which men have stated that doctrine in days gone by. To attempt here an adequate survey of the history of the Christian doctrine of Atonement is a task too great. The subject is so vast that it is almost a presumption to attempt to deal with it at all. It is almost requisite, however, that we should touch upon some of the theories that have been propounded to Christians in past ages as an explanation of the means whereby their redemption was effected.

In the first place, we are in possession of the New Testament writings, the most important source of information as to what the first disciples thought about the work of Christ in relation to sin. We need not attempt a classification of the various passages wherein the doctrine of Atonement is suggested if not defined. That work has been done over and over again. Every Nonconformist must be familiar with the forcible way in which the case is presented in Dr. Dale's *magnum opus*, or by Dr. Crawford or Macleod Campbell. Here we may content ourselves with the general statement that whatever our theory of the Atonement may be the Pauline, Petrine, and Johannine Epistles are full of statements which go to show that in the belief of the primitive Church the sufferings and death of our Lord had an immediate bearing upon the forgiveness of sins. I am at a loss to know how anyone can read the New Testament and come to any other conclusion. For the moment, therefore, we need seek to establish no more than this, that the work of Christ in relation to sin as set forth within the pages of the New Testament has been closely associated with His suffering and death. We are not told how this came to be the case, we are simply assured that it was the case. It is not a question of theory, but of fact.

After the apostolic period there ensues a time of darkness in the history of the nascent Christian society. We cannot say that we know much of what was happening during that period. But from the sub-apostolic age onward the case is different. Speaking broadly we may say that the consciousness of the nascent Christian Church is fairly well interpreted by the writings of the Fathers from Clement of Rome to Bernard of Clairvaux. The ante-Nicene writers, speaking generally, avoid giving any theory of the Atonement at all; they content themselves with stating the fact. Two exceptions may be cited—Origen and Irenæus. These two thinkers, though far apart in their spheres of labour, came near together in their theory of the redemptive work of Jesus Christ. According to their view man was held to have fallen under the dominion of Satan, and the Son of God by His sufferings paid a ransom to Satan in order that mankind should be freed from his power. The post-Nicene Fathers, for the most part, seem to have adopted this view without attempting to justify it. Amongst their statements we find the ideas that the Atonement was a ransom to Satan and yet a sacrifice to God. No explanation is offered of either ransom or sacrifice. Augustine anticipated the Christian thought of later times by suggesting that Christ's Atonement was part of an eternal purpose.

The next great name in Christian thought is Anselm, with whom Scholasticism may be said to begin. He rejected the ransom to Satan theory, saying as we should say now that Satan had no rights over humanity, and in place of this notion he advanced the idea of an infinite satisfaction for an infinite debt. He maintained that by man's sin the majesty of God had been offended, and yet that man was unable of himself to offer an adequate satisfaction for the offence. Hence in answer to the question *Cur Deus homo?* Anselm declared that the Son of God became man in order that He might offer the only satisfaction that could be considered adequate. God the Father, he contended, could not pardon sin without such an atonement.

Later mediæval opinion was divided as to the worth of Anselm's theory. The greatest of its critics was Abelard, who asked the very reasonable question how the guilt of mankind could be atoned for by the addition to that guilt which was involved in putting Christ to death. Even Abelard's famous opponent, St. Bernard, repudiated Anselm's contention that God was necessitated in such wise that He could not pardon sin without atonement, and fell back upon the pre-Anselmic theory of a satisfaction to Satan.

To us, nowadays, these explanations of a great article of Christian belief seem unsatisfactory, but it ought to be remembered that the men who held them were intellectually equal to the best that can be produced to-day. Their theories have failed because our habit of mind has changed. Theories are only husks; the kernel of truth lies within. All these theories had a common basis, or rather, a common thought underlay them, namely, that human guilt is so real that its removal requires more than the mere declaration that man is forgiven on repentance. It was felt that the reality of moral evil is so intractable that in some mysterious way its removal could only be purchased by the Passion of Deity.

When we come to the period of the Reformation the doctrine of Atonement receives a new emphasis. Roman Catholic doctrine on the subject agrees in the main with modern evangelical theology. Most of the Reformers, on the other hand, held and taught the doctrine of the total depravity of human nature, and introduced the idea that Christ bore the penal sufferings of sinners. Against this view Socinianism and allied systems of thought protested, but did so by going to the opposite extreme and declaring that in the Passion of Christ God enacted a drama, as it were, in the presence of humanity, and strove to win men's love by the exhibition of a suffering Saviour.

Modern thought has played around all these positions with the result that the doctrine of Atonement has either been pushed into the background altogether or has been presented in categories which the modern mind rejects.

One kind of evangelical theology seems to say that Christ died to save mankind from the penalty of sin. Salvation is regarded as the deliverance from the consequences of misdoing, and, while it would be hardly fair to say that evangelical Christianity as a whole is committed to this crude and one-sided view, it is certainly not too much to say that this is what the hearers of many evangelical appeals are given to understand.

A larger view of salvation has led many evangelical teachers to regard the fact of Atonement as of more importance than the theory. Butler, in the Analogy, makes this statement. Dr. Dale, in his preface to the work on the doctrine, says substantially the same thing, and appeals to experience as confirmation of the undoubted truth that the preaching of Christ crucified has set men free from the thraldom of sin and made a holy life possible. Another view is that presented by such mystical thinkers as William Law, who in his "Serious Call to a Devout and Holy Life," tells us that "to have a true idea of

Christianity we must not consider our blessed Lord as suffering in *our stead*, but as our *representative*, acting in our name, and with such particular merit as to make our joining with Him acceptable unto God."

From this position some preachers in our own day have taken the bolder course of omitting the objective side of the doctrine of Atonement altogether, and we are all familiar with the amount of hesitation, doubt, and bewilderment characteristic of honest religious teachers, who can find no place for the doctrine at all, and who think that the faithful declaration of the need of repentance and the certainty of God's pardoning love is sufficient for everyone. Yet history should count for something. Christian experience is cumulative, but surely aught that has exercised a strong formative influence upon Christian character through long periods of time has some claim to recognition and reverence. Common to all the foregoing statements of the doctrine of Atonement is some fact of experience. We should try to discover what it is.

When we say that the Christian doctrine of Atonement has persisted through the ages the very natural inquiry succeeds, *What is it that has persisted?* What is it that saints and theologians, from the first century to the nineteenth, have felt in common as to the need of a great work wrought by the Son of God for the doing away of human sin? It seems to me that this common element is the sense of guilt. The sense of guilt is a psychological fact which emerges at a certain stage of self-consciousness. It is not the worst men who feel the most guilty. A work of Christ is going on in the soul which is conscious of contrite sorrow for sin. Many of the noblest of the saints have passed through a period of anguish, self-reproach, and humiliation, at the beginning of their spiritual life. Men like Augustine, Cyprian, Bunyan, and Spurgeon have known this experience; their very holiness was the result of it. The sense of guilt, though not a universal fact, is a very general one, and we are justified in thinking that it has been a preliminary note of saintship in every age. It is this sense of guilt which has awakened men to the need of Atonement, and it is the discovery that the preaching of the fact of Atonement has the power to bring relief to the sense of guilt that has made men cling to the doctrine. Some explanation of the doctrine, therefore, based on the recognition that it comes as *a relief to the sense of guilt* and as a means of separation between a man and his evil past is the one we are waiting for.

II.—Suggestions toward a Theory.

We ought to note, in the first place, that with the appearance of Christ in the world there is coincident the emergence of a great spiritual need, the need of relief to the sense of guilt *when experienced*. It is not easy to say just where it begins or who has felt it and who has not. In some persons self-blame scarcely seems to awaken at all; in others it is fitful and incomplete, sometimes weaker, sometimes stronger, as the case may be. In others it exhibits itself as a tendency to lay stress on some evil deed or moral event in a life-history; while in others, again, it takes the form of sorrow for one's whole moral condition. The less important experiences may be passed over, but the deeper ones may not, for, paradox though it may seem, the very sense of short-coming or demerit which is a condition of true nobleness, a move toward holiness, is, if unrelieved, a fatal barrier from both. To feel oneself guilty is to be made capable of higher life, and yet unless one can somehow rise above that sense of guilt the higher life is for ever impossible. Here is the psychological fact that the doctrine of Atonement has in past ages successfully met, and the insistent need for the sake of which it ought to be preached to-day. I think we might quite legitimately say that unless the need has awakened in the soul of any man the doctrine will do him but little good and may be safely neglected; but if, on the other hand, there should be even one man, and only one in the whole world, who has passed through the deep experience of personal guilt, I should say that for him there ought to be a doctrine of Atonement to preach, otherwise his sense of guilt is a sentence of condemnation; he must remain where he is, without hope of attaining to the experience of holiness.

This statement may be objected to. On the one hand it is often maintained that for any sin, however great, the word of forgiveness and reconciliation is enough—a man needs no more; while on the other hand it is averred that the deed once done can never be undone, that the sinner must bear the consequences of his sin, and, what is more terrible, remain for ever associated with the crippling memory of it.

Let us look at these two assertions a little more closely. Is the word of forgiveness enough for any sin? Take the grosser ones and see. Suppose a man to be a murderer, or a thief on a large scale, or a liar, whose lies have affected the peace and happiness of other people in an appalling degree, and suppose that man to be capable at some stage of his moral history of realising the enormity of his crimes. What should we say about his chances of newness of life? His sense of guilt ought to lead to genuine penitence; his genuine penitence ought to assure him of God's forgiveness, but, as a matter of fact, does it? If it were possible for that man to kneel down in some quiet corner and rise again rejoicing that God had forgiven him for all the past we should not think much of the sincerity of his conversion. We should feel that his repentance was inadequate, and that he ought not to be absolved so easily from responsibility for all that he had been and done. What about the victims of his ruthless rapacity or unholy lust? What about the havoc he has wrought in happy homes and innocent lives? What about the long entail of misery, the far-reaching consequences of his wickedness—consequences that will continue long after the wretch feels himself forgiven? For such a case as this, then, evidently the word of forgiveness is not enough. If the culprit could convince himself that such was the case his repentance would not be genuine. By "not enough" I mean that even though his contrition be sincere something more is needed to *liberate* him from association with his own sinful past.

Nevertheless what are we to say to such a character if in better moments he should desire, not to escape punishment, but to put things right again? I know the answer that some might give. The sinner would be told to bear his own burden like a man, and not to expect that any person, human or divine, can set him free from responsibility for his own moral history. But the sinner knows all that without being told. So does anyone by watching the ordinary sequence of conduct and penalty; but to tell a sinner to bear the consequences of his sin is to ask him to do something beyond his power. One chief consequence of sin is more sin, and the first thought of many erring ones who are exhorted to change their mode of life is the desperately hopeless one that by sin they are already committed to sin and must go on in the dreary, dismal course that leads to further woe. Besides this the consequences of many a selfish deed are vaster and deeper and proceed farther than the sinner who committed the deed ever foresaw, and it is beyond his power to cope with them. Such considerations as these condemn many a man to a degraded, unholy life, who would be glad to bear any amount of pain if by so doing he could prevent the consequences of his sin from taking effect on other people.

Relief from the sense of guilt is therefore by no means so simple as it seems. Examine a little further the content of the sense of guilt.

1. In the first place, if a man feels himself to be really guilty he feels that in some way *his soul is under condemnation*. Some would aver that this is the same thing as to say that the sinner feels himself to be under the wrath of God, but I do not think such a feeling is present in every case of contrition. It were better to say the wrongdoer feels that the general *rightness* of things is against him. For a man to persist in wrong when he knows it to be wrong is to be condemned by the mysterious inner law of his own being. He may not stay to analyse his feelings, but he knows perfectly

well that the obligation to do right brings with it certain sanctions and penalties which do not defer their whole operation to some future period; they set to work at once and compel the sinner to feel that the general rightness of things, the voice of conscience, the law of life, the worth of progress, the sweet accents of love, the holy will of God, are all against him.

2. In addition to this there is the fact already hinted at, namely, that *every sinner feels himself to be permanently associated with his own evil deeds*. Suppose that a man has committed a great sin, such, for instance, as the betrayal of a trust. If that sin becomes known to society the sinner will be punished, not only by the censures of his fellows, but by their remembrance of his action. He will always be pointed at as the man who did such and such things in such and such a year. Even though the world does not know of the misdeed his experience ought not to be much different. He will carry his hell about with him. He will be prevented from undertaking many a worthy enterprise

because of his own association with a deed that disqualifies him for work that he would have undertaken quite willingly had his history been pure. He will be, as it were, chained to the corpse of his own past, and in consequence restrained from forms of activity in which he would be otherwise qualified to shine.

3. Of more moment is it, however, to think that not only activity but character is robbed by the association with sin. *The chief penalty of sin is inhibition from good.* To the man who has fallen holiness is a forbidden land. The dreadfulness of the sinner's lot consists not so much in the fact that he must be punished for his sin as that he must be for ever shut off from experiences that he deems possible to others. If, for instance, a man has been a convict it would be out of character for him to seek to be the leader, counsellor, and guide of a great society or a great nation. The experience which made him a convict acts as an inhibition. He can never come to feel as the trusted and revered masters of men do. Society will have none of him, and even if it would he

can never bring himself to try to feel as a man would who has not sinned his sin.

4. A fourth note of the sense of guilt is *man's inability to atone for his sin*. He cannot put things right again, however much he may desire to do so, for the consequences of every sinful act lie beyond the control of the sinner. A man may repent with all his might; he may be quite willing to bear in his own person a penalty appropriate to his own misdoing, but what he cannot do is to remove from other people's characters and fortunes the influences that he has set going. Mark, it is not the fear of punishment that is the chief element in this experience, it is simply the feeling of inability to gather up the consequences and bear them in his own person.

We ought also to remark in this connection that it is not only deeds but thoughts, feelings, and disposition that have far-reaching consequences. It were fitting that some men should repent of what they *are* rather than of what they have done.

These notes of the sense of guilt put

together form a very real experience, an experience which becomes clamant. What is asked for is the severance of the entail between man and his sin. If the Gospel of Christ cannot provide a remedy for this, then there is one order of human experience for which that Gospel is inadequate.

It is noteworthy that the sense of guilt as we have now stated it is the product of the influence of Jesus Christ in the world. Nothing precisely like it is to be found apart from that influence. There is a great difference in the tone of mind exhibited by the Psalmists and the Christian saints respectively. The Psalmists lay stress upon deeds rather than dispositions, and deep as is their feeling of personal demerit it lacks something of the contrite sorrow for sin which expresses itself in charity toward others and severity toward self. I have no wish to underrate the force and beauty of the language of contrition contained in the Psalms, but what I am desirous to advance is that the contrition caused by the personal influence of Jesus Christ in the world strikes a deeper note and contains an ingredient not previously present in any age. But to say that Jesus deepened the self-consciousness of the race in such a way as to add a new element to contrition, without contributing any higher hope of rescue, is to say that His influence caused the emergence of a new need without providing a satisfaction for it. As Professor Van Dyke says: "It was Jesus of Nazareth who illuminated the moral evil in the world most deeply and clearly. He showed its spring, its secret workings, and the power which lies behind it. . . . The sinlessness of Jesus comforts us little unless it has some remedial bearing upon our sins." The Christian doctrine of Atonement is the only remedy which has ever been propounded to the world to deal with the psychological fact of guilt. It satisfies a Christ-awakened need.

The key to a theory of the doctrine seems to me to be supplied, firstly, by acceptance of the hypothesis that *the origin of moral evil is in God*, and, secondly, by the Christian doctrine of the Person of Christ. If Christ be the Eternal

Son of God, that side of the Divine nature which has gone forth in creation, if He contains humanity, and is present in every act and article of human experience, then, indeed, we have a light upon the fact of redemption. For Jesus is thus seen to be associated with the existence of the primordial evil which has its origin in God. Without acquaintance with evil man could never have known good, while submission to evil after the good is clearly seen becomes sin. We may say there would be no sin if there were no evil bias, yet without that evil bias holiness were impossible, for innocence is not holiness, it is good unrealised. Evil is an experience for the sake of the far-off holiness it makes possible. The eternal Son, the going-forth of God, must therefore be associated with responsibility for the bias without which neither guilt nor sainthood could have come into being. He, and He only, therefore, can sever the entail between man and his responsibility for personal sin. Christ has not *sinned* in man, but takes responsibility for that experience of evil into which humanity is born, and the yielding to which constitutes sin. Thus the first link in the entail of guilt becomes broken.

But, it may be advanced, if this is so would it not have been enough for Christ to have revealed it to the world, and, assuming responsibility for the origin of moral evil, have remitted the sins of all who sought forgiveness? Would it not have been enough to tell men the truth, and by the telling set them free? The answer to this inquiry is that this is precisely what Christ usually did in the days of His flesh. "Thy sins be forgiven thee," "Go in peace and sin no more," were expressions often upon His lips. Neither did He explain the mystery of His own sufferings for sin, but His references to His Passion, and the deep and solemn meaning that He evidently attached to it, the institution of the Lord's Supper and the agony of Gethsemane, though unexplained are evidences of a deeper work necessitated by the fact of human guilt. And, as we have just tried to show, it is not a work that man feels no need of. Many men feel not only that they want to be forgiven, but that the consequences of misdoing are somehow gathered up in the purposes of God and dealt with. So they are, for Christ suffers them. He not only knows but feels and shares the woe of the world. The going-forth of God in creation may be explained in two ways. He goes forth to suffer and suffers in man; He creates evil that man may know good. The Eternal Son in Whom humanity is contained is therefore a sufferer since creation began. This mysterious Passion of Deity must continue until redemption is consummated and humanity restored to God. *Thus every consequence of human ill is felt in the experience of Christ.* No single human being can endure more of those consequences than fall to his lot for the sake of discipline : Christ endures them all. Calvary is the point at which we can touch this great mystery. In the life of the historical Jesus, in the garden of Gethsemane, in the cross of Christ, the clouds parted, as it were, and the world obtained a glimpse of a great experience that lies behind. By taking responsibility for the origin of moral evil Christ severs the entail between the penitent and his guilt, frees him from association with it, removes the barrier or inhibition between him and good, and makes holiness possible, while at the same time His Passion, a mystery we can only touch at the cross, contains all the consequences of human sin. Christ is the circumference of the life of humanity. Part of His Passion is lived in every suffering child of man, but a deeper part is lived beyond and beneath the range of any individual human experience. All the consequences of human wrong-doing are consummated and wrought out in His experience. "Surely He hath borne our griefs and carried our sorrows; the chastisement of our peace was upon Him, and with His stripes we are healed."

It is not only the result of human deeds, but also the result of human character that is present in the experience of Christ. There is a very good Buddhist term that stands for the total result of the life and character of any individual man. That term is *karma*. It means substantially the result of a man's life taken as a whole. If we can suppose that every deed we have done, every thought that has passed through our minds is gathered up, and that the sum total of our influence in the world continues even after we have passed beyond it, we may say that our *karma* necessitates the Passion of Christ. It is *karma* that the sinner dreads; it is the evil in his *karma* that he desires to get rid of, and it is just this evil that no repentance can delete. The most glorious fact in the Christian system is the fact that Christ, Who contains humanity, permits the *karma* to work its full effect upon Him, and by so doing purifies, not the individual only, but in the fulness of time the race in such wise that the higher experience of good remains while the guilt of sin is destroyed. It is in this sense that we can understand the mystical text, "He hath made Him to be sin for us Who knew no sin, that we might become the righteousness of God in Him."

II.

BY F. W. FARRAR, D.D.,
Dean of Canterbury.

ALL clergymen who do not live in a dreamland of religious unrealities, but are really cognisant of the tone of thought which prevails in the wide Christian world, must be aware that there are methods of presenting the doctrine of the Atonement which put a terrible stumbling-block in the path of thousands of those who think and feel for themselves, and are not content to take at second-hand what may be presented to them as "the scheme of salvation." Many able and intellectual men, entirely discontent with the placid and autocratic shibboleths of very imperfectly - equipped teachers, have—as a distinguished public man once expressed it to me—"thought out the fundamental truths of religion for themselves, and are content to let the clergy talk." Others, and not unfrequently women of sincere and tender souls, feel a shock to their moral sense from many statements which profess to explain the necessity for the death of Christ. They are shocked at the notion of a justice by which "a criminal can suffer penalty by deputy and have sentence executed upon him by substitute."* With a feeling of something like anguish, they find themselves so completely in disaccord with what they hear from the pulpit, as even to have an agonising doubt whether they are not forced to regard themselves as "heretics." If I am not mistaken the survival of doctrinal crudities, no longer tenable with the truths brought home to us by the light of advancing knowledge, is a *chief*, if it be not the sole, cause on the one hand for widespread disbelief, and on the other for that aloofness from the work and worship of the Church of Christ, which is one of the ominous features of our age.

It will be, of course, impossible in one brief paper to go to the root of this vast question, on which, in almost every age, so many ponderous folios have been written. It will, above all, be

* Mozley, *University Sermons*, p. 184.

impossible to examine all the texts and every metaphor on which have been built the vast inverted pyramids of theological error and presumption. This, however, we may say at once. According to the wise rule of St. Augustine, "*Scriptura est sensus Scripturæ*"—Scripture *is* what Scripture *means*. It is futile, in treating of such a subject as the Atonement, to rely only on " the ever-widening spiral *ergo* from the narrow aperture of single texts ";—especially when our endless inferences from those texts run directly counter to the plain teaching of other texts, and to the general revelation of God in Holy Scripture, and by His Spirit to the souls of men. It is especially pernicious to press, to all sorts of remote logical consequences, metaphors which were only intended to touch on one aspect of the truth, and to illustrate its bearing upon a single point. In the remarks which follow we shall see that this has again and again been done. It is well for us to remember that, since God is infinite and man finite— since "it has not pleased Almighty God to reveal to us the plan of salvation in dialectics"

—it is often an idle and misleading effort to present the great fact of man's salvation in systems of theological scholasticism. We may at once sweep aside as utterly false not a little of what has been dogmatically announced thousands of times by popular preachers, as though it were the only "orthodoxy," and as though to disbelieve it were wicked atheism!

For instance,

I. We reject as utterly false, and absolutely contrary to the whole teaching of Scripture, those presentations of the Atonement which represent GOD THE FATHER as full of wrath and vengeance, which was only averted by the tenderness of GOD THE SON. The language of the Augsburgh Conference, that Christ died "*ut reconciliaret nobis Patrem,*" and of our own Fourth Article, that "He suffered, was crucified, dead, and buried, *to reconcile the Father unto us,*" may be capable of being rightly explained. But this is *not* the language of Scripture, which invariably says that Christ died " to reconcile (not *God* to us, but) *us* to

God."* When we read such lines as those of Sir Henry Wotton:—

> One rosy drop from Jesu's heart,
>   Was worlds of seas to *quench God's ire*,

or as those of Dr. Watts:—

> Rich were the drops of Jesu's blood
>   That *calmed God's frowning face*,
>   That sprinkled o'er the burning throne,
>   And turned the wrath to grace:—

or when we read such ghastly and revolting anthropomorphism as the phrase of Dr. Cumming, that Jesus "wiped away the red anger-spot from the brow of God";—or of Professor Parkes, that "God drew His sword upon Calvary, and slew His only Son";—or of Mr. Spurgeon, that "Christ took the cup in both His hands, and at one tremendous draught of love drank damnation dry";—or that "the *feud* between God and the poor soul need not be continued," because "it would be injustice to lay the sin upon the substitute and also upon the sinner";—when, I say, we read such

---

* 2 Cor. v. 18, 19, " Of God, who reconciled *us* to Himself "; " God was in Christ, reconciling the world unto Himself." (*Comp.* Rom. v. 10, 11; Col. i. 21.)

phrases, they seem to be absolutely deplorable if they be placed side by side with the revelation that "God is Love," or with such passages as "I trust in the MERCY of God for ever and ever." An American murderer, fortified in this coarse travesty by his prison chaplain, said to the multitude from the scaffold, "I hold up Christ's blood between me and the flaming face of God." "The Scriptures," says Dr. Campbell, "do *not* represent the love of God to man as the effect, and the Atonement as the cause, *but just the contrary :* the love of God as *the cause* and *the Atonement as the effect*." "God's whole nature," said Archbishop Magee, "is one great impulse to what is best." Even as far back as the fifth century the Pope, St. Leo the Great, in contradistinction from the crudities of many modern preachers, with far deeper truth and wisdom, said of the Father and the Son: "*One* is the kindness of their mercy as the sentence of their justice nor is there any division in action where there is no diversity in will." Much, perhaps, of the error which I am combating may be due to the myriad-fold-repeated phrase that God forgives us *"for Christ's sake."* But although a true meaning may be attached to that expression, it is *not* the expression of St. Paul, who uses the far deeper and true phrase that "God *in Christ* forgave us."* The statement that God did anything *for Christ's sake* does not once occur in the New Testament. That God *in Christ* saves us, according to His mercy, is a very different conception.

II. Again, although volumes have been written to support the theory or inference of "*vicarious punishment,*" many forms in which that theory has been stated are dishonouring to God, and revolt the unsophisticated conscience of man. " The doctrine of the Atonement," says Mozley, " rises altogether to another level; it parts company with the gross and irrational conception of mere naked material substitution of one person for another, and it takes its stand

---

* Eph. iv. 32. The proper rendering of 1 John ii. 12 is " *On account of His name,*" which has quite a different meaning. (*Comp.* John xx. 31.)

upon the power of love." That Christ was *substituted* to suffer for us—in order to offer, so to speak, a mechanical equivalent for the guilty human race, and so to reconcile (?) God's justice with His mercy, as though justice and mercy were at internecine war with each other in the mind of God—is a view which contradicts the whole teaching of Scripture. The Bible *never* represents the Atonement as effecting any change in the mind of God. The doctrine of Scripture is that of *free forgiveness*, not *vicarious punishment*. In Gal. iii. 13, 14, St. Paul, using one of the many different expressions in which he tried to set forth the truths of man's reconciliation to God in Christ, says that He " became a curse for us "; but he expressly *omits* the words of Deut. xxi. 23, " a curse *of God*," which would have been the words *most* required by the theory that God was requiring Christ to bear a penalty in our stead. Are those who preach these crude views to ignore the fact that neither " *vicarious* " nor " *substitution*," nor " *satisfaction*," nor " *expiation*," nor " *imputed righteousness* " so much as once occur in the New Testament? Even the word "imputed" does not occur in the Revised Version. Is it an insignificant fact that the word αντὶ—which would be required by the theory of vicarious substitution—is *never* used of Christ's death for us, but always ὑπὲρ or περὶ "on our behalf"?* Is it nothing that it is not once stated in the New Testament that Christ "saved us from the *penalty* of our sins"; or that His death was "a penalty" at all? There is only one chapter of the Old Testament which, even in the way of metaphor can be pressed into the conception that Christ died as our substituted equivalent.† Hengstenberg says that this chapter "sounds through the whole New Testament" in this sense. Yet, so far is this from being the case, that where it is directly referred to by St. Matthew—the one Evangelist who dwells most systematically on Messianic prophecy—he is so far from understanding the language of "the Evangelical Prophet" in *this* sense, that he quotes it as having been directly fulfilled by Christ's *works*

* On Matt. xx. 28, see *infra*. † Is. liii. 4, 5.

of healing mercy, which showed that by His sympathy He shared our sorrows. For, after telling of the deliverance of many demoniacs and sick people he expressly adds, "*that it might be fulfilled which was spoken by Isaiah the Prophet, saying, Himself took our infirmities and bare our diseases.*"

III. Nor again is it right to interpret the Death of Christ as the exact counterpart to *the Mosaic sacrifices* of the old Dispensation. It has been assumed that the victims offered on the Jewish altar were looked upon as reconciling the offender to God by the death of the innocent on behalf of the guilty; yet a deeply reverent and careful theologian says "in the whole Jewish ritual *there is no trace of such an idea,*" and "if no such idea attached to the *symbol,* we may be very sure no such idea attaches to the *reality* to which the symbol pointed.* The Jewish sacrifices were

---

* Archdeacon Norris, "Rudiments of Theology," p. 129. Similarly, Bishop Westcott says that in the Præ Mosaic sacrifices " there is *no trace of the idea of vicarious substitution, nor of propitiation (comp.* Mic. vi. 7)," Epistle to the Hebrews, p. 287.

offered as sin-offerings, burnt offerings and peace-offerings; the two latter represented the conceptions of self-surrender and thanksgiving; and the sin-offering symbolised the oblation, or carrying away (נָשָׂא) of, defilement. Just as ἀντὶ "*in the place of*," is not used in the New Testament to support any theory of substitution, but ὑπὲρ and περὶ, so the Hebrew word for "*instead of*" *(tachath)* is never used in the Old Testament of the offered victim; and, although Christ is in the New Testament called "the Lamb of God," it is to this day disputed whether the reference be to the Paschal lamb, or to the figure of the lamb in *Isaiah*, or a type of Divine patience and suffering. The words of St. Peter, again—which should be rendered "He carried up our sins in His own body on to the tree"—have no sacrifical sense, as the verb ἀνήνεγκεν has in James ii. 21; for the notion of " offering up SINS as a sacrifice " is simply absurd. And if the sin-offerings had been regarded as substitutes for the offender, how could they possibly have been eaten, as they were? That single fact shatters the whole false theory. The Jewish sin-offerings were not even intended to atone for sin in general, but only for certain specified sins; and if they had possessed the sort of validity which modern inferences have attributed to them, they would not have been so sweepingly disparaged by the almost unanimous voice of the Prophets.* "I will have mercy and not sacrifice" is the favourite quotation of our Lord.† But, as has been said by a Jewish theologian, Prof. Israel Abrahams, "Vicariousness is a conception utterly foreign to the Pentateuch."

IV. Entirely mistaken notions have probably been created in the minds, especially of Western theologians, by the many references to the saving effects of "the Blood of Christ." The expression has often been glibly expanded into endless inferences by preachers and hymn-writers, who had not the remotest conception

---

* 1 Sam. xv. 22; Psalms li. 16; l. 8, 9, 14, 23. Isaiah i. 11. Amos v. 21, 22. Hosea vi. 6. Micah vi. 6-8, &c.
† Matt. ix. 13.; xii. 7.

that the sacred connotations of the word
"Blood" among the Jews were the *absolute
antithesis* of those which we attach to it. The
Blood of Christ "cleanses our consciences from
dead works to serve a living God" (Heb ix.
14), because "the Blood of Christ" is the
symbol, *not of His death*, but of His Eternal
Life. The Blood, we read, as far back as Gen.
ix. 4, "*is the Life.*"* "The Blood of Christ" is
"not simply the price by which the redeemed
were purchased, but the power by which they
were quickened so as to be capable of belonging
to God." "It is Christ that died," says St.
Paul, "*Yea, rather*, that was raised from the
dead, who also maketh intercession for us"
(Rom. viii. 34). The lessons of sacrifice in
the Old Testament were not those of substitution of innocent for guilty, but of "service,

* See Deut. xii. 23, Lev. xvii. 11, "the life" (*nephesh*
"**soul**") of the flesh is in the blood. . . The Blood
atones through the Life. "It will be evident," says Bishop
Westcott (on 1 John i. 7), "that while the thought of
Christ's blood (as shed) includes all that is involved in
Christ's death, the Death of Christ, on the other hand
expresses only the initial part of the whole conception of
Christs's Blood. The Blood always includes the thought
of the life preserved and active beyond death."

cleansing, consecration, fellowship." The sin-offerings did not even deal with serious moral offences at all, but simply with ceremonial pollutions, some of ignorance, and a few specified offences (Lev. iv. 1ff; v. 15 ff; vi. 1, 7; xix 20). They were, as a rule, killed by the offerer, not by the priest, and "no stress was laid on death or suffering." The stress was laid on the *sprinkling* of the blood, because the blood was regarded as the essential life.* When we are told that "*in* the blood of Jesus we have boldness to enter into the holy place" (Heb. x. 19) the meaning is that the Life of Christ, shared by us and imparted to us by the Spirit, has given us consecration and ratified an eternal covenant. Hence the New Testament dwells far more on the blood of Christ, which represents the energy of His true human life, than on the death which was necessary to make that blood available for our salvation.

V. But it will perhaps be said that whatever significance may attach to the other sacrifices,

---

* "It is the blood that maketh atonement for the soul." (Lev. xvii. 11.)

at any rate the ceremonies of the Day of Atonement point to vicarious substitution. I will not here enter into the question whether those ceremonies were any part of the original Mosaic Law, or whether they only originated after the Exile; but in any case the fact that there is not a single allusion to them in a thousand years of Jewish history must make it very doubtful whether they could have had this significance. But, apart from this, how is the conception of "vicarious substitution" compatible with the fact that the high priest of that day " made an atonement " for the holy place, and the tabernacle, and the altar? High Jewish authorities tell us that the dismissal of the scapegoat to the evil demon Azazel in the wilderness meant no more than what Micah meant when he said, " Thou will cast all our sins into the depths of the sea." The ordinary sin offerings had *already* been offered, and " there was *no notion* of physically transferring the guilt of the nation on to the head of the scapegoat."

VI. Another common mistake, which has

been indeed habitual for centuries, is to place the death of Christ in a wrong perspective by isolating it from His life, and speaking of it far too exclusively as the cause of our redemption. "Christ's death," says the late Dr. Littledale, "in ancient Christian theology did not pervade by any means so much space as it has done for several centuries past, but it was regarded as a single incident—of transcendent importance and value indeed, but still only a single incident—in the great chain of events from the Incarnation to the Ascension." "Non *Mors* sed *voluntas* placuit, sponte morientis," says St. Bernard. If we are guided by the teaching of Christ Himself, He says, "The *words* which I speak unto you, *they* are spirit and they are life." He did not speak by any means habitually, or exclusively, of His death, but always represented it as a part of, and in one sense the culmination of, His voluntary self-sacrifice. The instincts of the unsophisticated Christian heart have fixed upon the Parable of the Prodigal Son as one of the divinest revelations uttered by the lips of love; and in the Parable of the Prodigal Son what allusion is there to "imputed merits" or "vicarious satisfaction" and "forensic accommodations"? It is remarkable that while Christ was all in all to the primitive Christians—while He was their glory and joy and crown of rejoicing—they never for four or five centuries represented the Cross or passion in their catacombs or on their sarcophagi. Partly they regarded it as a positive and daring irreverence to do so, and partly their thoughts were absorbed in the Ever-living, the glorified, the Eternal, the Ever-present Christ. As was the case with the Christians of the Apostolic age, " the fellowship with Christ's sufferings,' was transfigured into the *exultation* (ἀγαλλίασις) over His triumph, and the brief agonies of crucifixion were only contemplated in the light of the session at the right hand of God. That sort of morbid "deification of pain," which has entered so largely into the religion of externalism and formal superstition, has no place in the New Testament or in Scriptual and primitive Christianity. The early Christians were rather pervaded by the realisation of joy, and felt the force of the repeated exhortation of St. Paul, "Rejoice evermore." Crucifixes and stigmata, emotional weeping over the five wounds, and kneeling before the Stations of the Cross, and elaborate attempts to recall our Lord's physical agonies on the Cross—to which all the four Gospels only allude in the single word, "I thirst"—are the product, not of primitive Christianity, but of mediæval superstition.

VII. It is a reflection at once strange and sad that, because theologians have not been content to accept Christ's atonement as a transcendent fact, they have in all ages fallen into error respecting it, and have tried to represent it as a juridical transaction. It is not a revelation which we can explain in systematically logical forms, because it is mainly presented in varying metaphors, which admit of varying interpretations, and those metaphors indicate its results as regards us men and our salvation, not the incomprehensible mystery of its relation to

God.* Much as *The Epistle to the Hebrews* dwells on Christ's sacrifice, yet, on its eternal and transcendental side the writer has nothing to say more than in the most general terms that "it *became* God, it *was fitting* that God in bringing many sons to glory, should make the author of their salvation perfect through sufferings" (Heb. ii. 10); and again, that because every high priest offers gifts and sacrifices, "it is *necessary* that this High Priest also have somewhat to offer" (Heb. viii. 3).

VIII. One of the four metaphors under which the effects of Christ's death are represented to us is ransom (λύτρον, λύτρωσις, Matt. xx. 28, Mark x. 45, 1 Tim. ii. 6; ἀγοράζειν, ἐεγοράζειν, 1 Cor. vi. 20, vii. 22, Gal. iii. 13, iv. 5, Rev. v. 9, xiv. 3). The words "ransom," "redemption" express the effects of Christ's work in delivering us from the bondage of sin, of Satan and spiritual death. This was "achieved" or "purchased" for us

---

* "Definite statements respecting the relation of Christ either to God or man are but human figures transferred to a subject which is beyond speech or thought."—Jowett, *Romans II.*, 482.

—the metaphor is derived from the purchase of slaves—by the life and death of Christ just as the analogous Hebrew words are applied in the Old Testament to the deliverance of Israel from Egypt. Our Lord when He spoke of giving His life as "a ransom for many"* simply expresses the truth that we were the slaves of sin, and that by His life and death He delivered us from that bondage. The tendency to systematise led Irenæus to suggest the question "to whom was the ransom paid?" and to answer that it was paid to the Devil! This false conception, involving the grossest anthropomorphism, was elaborated by Origen and continued dominant in the Church for nearly a thousand years. It was exploded by St. Anselm, who, in his *Cur Deus Homo*, exposed the monstrous notion that God could be under a formal obligation to recognise the claims of the Devil. St. Anselm, however, holding that the ransom was paid by Christ *to*

* λύτρον ἀντὶ πολλῶν, Matt. xx. 28; but that the word ἀντὶ has no *exceptional* significance is shown by the fact that, when St. Paul refers to the metaphor, he uses ὑπέρ (1 Tim. ii. 6).

God, elaborated the hardly less erroneous conception of a juristic transaction, and of an exact substituted equivalent, which in various forms has lasted till the present day, although the idea is only deduced by the unlimited expansion of general metaphors. We know that Christ died for us men and for our salvation, "that He might bring us to God."* Any attempt to *explain* the exact nature and method of this transcendently Divine compassion is a futile endeavour to be wise above what is written, and to translate the language of emotion into the rigidity of syllogisms, and of rapturous thanksgiving into that of rigid scholasticism. Scripture in its various elements resembles a mosaic; and as far back as the second century St. Irenæus said that it was always possible to break up the mosaic of a king, and reconstruct it into the semblance of a dog or of a fox.

IX. Two other substantives are used of the Atonement, one is καταλλαγή, which was rendered "Atonement" in the Authorised

* Rom. v. 6-8; 1 Pet. iii. 18.

Version, but—since it was no longer universally recognised that atonement means *at-one*-ment— is rendered *"reconciliation"* in the Revised Version. It occurs in Rom. v. 11, xi. 15, 2 Cor. v. 18, 19. It explains itself, if only we bear in mind, that it is not a reconciliation of *God to us*, but of *us to God*.

X. The word *"propitiation"* ($\dot{\iota}\lambda\alpha\sigma\mu\dot{o}s$) is used by St. John alone in 1 John ii. 2, iv. 10, and the verb "to propitiate" only in Heb. ii. 17, except in the prayer of the publican, "God *be merciful* (*lit.* 'be propitiated') to me the sinner" (Luke xviii. 13). In this passage Christ is represented as a faithful high priest "to propitiate (not 'God,' but) the sins of the people." It is noticeable that the verb does not refer to a single act but to a continuous process, and that " the propitiation acts *on that which alienates God* and not on God, whose love is unchanged throughout." The propitiation, as St. Chrysostom and other Fathers say, is the reconciliation of us to God by purging away our sins; and in fact "to sanctify," "to cleanse" and "to propitiate" are all three used in the

Greek version as translations of the Hebrew equivalent *Kippur*. Bishop Westcott points out that in classical Greek the verb " to propitiate " is used with the *accusative* of the *person* propitiated; but in the New Testament it is used with the dative of the *person*, and the *accusative* of the *sin !* "It contains the notion *not* of *appeasing one often in anger*, but of altering the character of that which interposes . . . an inevitable obstacle to fellowship. The propitiation, when it is applied to the sinner, neutralises the sin" (Luke viii. 13, Heb. ii. 17). The author of *The Epistle to the Hebrews* uses τὸ ἱλαστήριον "*the propitiatory*" as the representative of the Hebrew *Kapporeth*, the *covering* or mercy-seat over the Ark. Even on *Rom.* iii. 25 some commentators, from Origen down to Dr. Vaughan, take the word in the sense of "mercy-seat." It will be seen at once how far removed are these conceptions from the inferences which have been drawn from this almost isolated word. The Atonement is the true mercy-seat—the angel-guarded covering of the broken tables of the Law. The glory-cloud of the Divine Presence rests between the outstretched wings of its golden cherubim, and it is ever sprinkled with the cleansing blood which typifies the new and Divine life.

XI. The effects of the Atonement are also sometimes represented as the discharge of a debt, as in Gal. v. 3, 2 Cor. v. 21, Tit. ii. 14, 1 Pet. iii. 18; but this conception cannot be represented in a single word.

XII. We come, then, to the general conclusion that the metaphors of Scripture describe the Atonement in *its effects* as regards ourselves; not in its essence, which surpasses our powers of understanding. *Ignorando cognoscitur*. "Scripture," says Bishop Butler, "has left this matter of the satisfaction of Christ mysterious, left somewhat in it unrevealed," so that "all conjectures about it must be, if not evidently absurd, at least uncertain." The three great creeds of Christendom carefully avoid all attempts to express it by any rigid formula of explanation. They do not build figurative illustrations into solid edifices of dogmatic theology. They are content to indicate, as we should be content to know, that "after a certain admirable manner"—but *how* we are unable to define—it was in its *effects*, a full, perfect and sufficient redemption, propitiation and satisfaction for all the sins of the whole world, both original and actual, and there is none other satisfaction for sin but that alone." And in this sense, we may say with Hooker, "Let it be counted folly or fury or frenzy or whatsoever, it is our wisdom and our comfort; we care for no knowledge in the world but this, that man hath sinned and God hath suffered; that God hath made Himself the sin of men, and that men are made the righteousness of God."*

* 2 Cor. v. 21. Hooker *Serm.* II. 6.

III.

BY P. T. FORSYTH M.A., D.D.,
Cambridge.

I.—Negative.

"Back to Christ" is a most necessary movement in every unsettled age; but the Reformers' version of it is the true one. If the word is taken in spiritual earnest it means "back to the Cross," and back to the Cross means not only back to the moral principle of sacrifice, but back to the religious principle of expiation. Moreover, to go back to a principle which is really the act of a person is to go back to a power. And the one power the Church needs to have revived is that power of personal faith which gathers about the reality—and the experience—of justification. There is no real revival of the Church which does not revive that.

It is impossible in this region to separate religion from theology. A religion of sympathy may be so separated, but then it is not, strictly speaking, a religion. It might be Positivism, or some other fraternity. But a religion of forgiveness must be a religion of theology. It is our answer, not to a human need, but to a Divine revelation.

If the faith of the Church is take a new departure it must proceed from a new and practical grasp of revelation; and of the revelation which deals with the central human situation—the situation of sin and guilt. It is a faith and revelation which are concentrated in an Atonement.

The mind and soul of the Church returns to this perennial interest. The Church must always adjust its compass at the Cross. But in so returning it does not simply retrace the steps or tread the round of those that have gone before. There is a deepening evolution of human thought in this regard. The efforts to pluck the heart from its mystery are not a series of assaults renewed with blind and dogged courage on an impregnable hold. They form the stages of a long spiritual movement of slow battle, of arduous illumination and severe conquest. We have gone, *e.g.*, through the 'moral theory,' and come out at the other side, not where we went in. To this movement little or nothing is contributed by the inferior branches of human thought or knowledge. The revelation of God in the Cross of Christ is its own reforming principle and its own cleansing light. Nothing gained in anthropology, psychology, or philosophy can really do more than remove the misconceptions which they themselves created in their first blundering stages. The Cross is its own interpreter, and its own reformer, and its own sanctifier. It is its own principle, its own corrective, its own deliverer from misconstruction rational or irrational. It is its own evidence to our moral need. No conclusions of anthropology, for instance, about a historic fall, or the connection of sin and physical death, affect the matter. The need of Atonement does not rest on an historic fall, but on the reality of present and corporate guilt. And the fact of it rests on an experience as real as any which forms the basis of science. The Christian

mind, moved and lightened by the Holy
Ghost, does not rotate but march. And the
progress is no less sure because it is neither
continuous nor direct. We have much to
drop on the route as a condition of getting
home. We have to save truth by losing it,
though it seem part of our soul. We shed
the husk to grow the tree. And in this matter
of Atonement some things are clearly learnt
to be wrong, some are as clearly found to be
true as we move from faith to faith.

1. We have outgrown the idea that God has
to be reconciled. We see, as we never did
before, how unscriptural that is. We know
that the satisfaction made by Christ, no less
than the sacrifices of the old law, flowed from
the grace of God, and did not go to procure it.

2. We have outgrown the idea that Redemption cost the Father nothing, that He had only
to receive the payment, or even the sacrifice,
which the Son made. We realise more clearly
that the Son could not suffer without the Father
suffering. We realise that forgiveness did cost,
that it was not a matter of course to paternal

indulgence, that it involved conditions of sorrow which were not confined either to Christ or to man, that a forgiveness which cost the forgiver nothing would lack too much in moral value or dignity to be worthy of holy love or rich in spiritual effect.

3. We have outgrown the idea that Christ took our punishment in the quantitative sense of the word. What He offered was not an *equivalent*. So also there can be no imputation as transfer of quantitative merit. We are agreeing to see that what fell upon Him was not the equivalent punishment of sin, but the due judgment of it, its condemnation. But we are also returning to see that what He bore *was* sin's condemnation, and not a mere sympathetic suffering. He did not indeed bear our guilt in the sense of a vicarious repentance. That for His holiness was impossible. He who was made sin for us could never be made sinful, nor, being made a curse for us, was He accursed. But yet what He bore was much more than the *Weltschmerz*, the human travail; it was the condemnation of sin in the flesh.

4. We are only just escaping from the modern and sentimental idea of love which found no difficulty placed by the holy law of God's nature in His way of forgiveness. It is an immoral love which has no moral hesitation about mercy. There are conditions to be met which reside, not in man, but in the very nature of God Himself, and so of human dignity. The key to the whole situation on this question lies in some words I have already quoted in public.

"The dignity of man would be better assured if he were shattered on the inviolability of this holy law than if for his mere happy existence it were ignored."

I hope that we are beyond the idea that punishment is an arbitrary ordinance of God, that the conjunction of sin and suffering is the result of a mere decree, and that the same will which decreed it can dissolve it at His kind pleasure. We realise, in our moral progress under the Christian revelation, that the law which ruins the sinner is as eternal and holy in the nature of God as the passion to make him a saint. And we have in the whole New Testament a standard of Divine love which is truer than those domestic analogues so dear to a theology popularised among great classes with no interest in life higher than the affections. There are some to whose experience the parable of the prodigal means more than the death of Christ.

5. We have outgrown also the other extreme —that forgiveness cost so much that it was impossible to God till justice was appeased and mercy set free by the blood of Christ.

6. We have further left the idea behind that the satisfaction of Christ was made either to God's wounded honour or to His punitive justice. And we see with growing and united clearness that it was made by obedience rather than by suffering. There is a vast difference between suffering as a condition of Atonement and suffering as the thing of positive worth in it, what gives it its value. We are beyond the idea that there was any saving value in the mere act of dying, apart from the spiritual manner of it.

It is not a mere fact, but the person in it, that can mediate between soul and soul. It is true the effect would not have been won if Christianity had been complete in the Sermon on the Mount and Christ had passed to heaven from the Mount of Transfiguration; but not because He would not have paid the death penalty, but only because a vital and terminal portion of human experience would have been excluded from acknowledging in Him the righteousness of God. The saving value both of His sorrow and death came from a holy obedience, owning, in His most intense and extreme actuality of life — viz., agony and death—the righteousness of the broken law. The law was a law of hungering holiness, and the submission and sacrifice were not to mere clamant justice or Divine wrath.

The wrath of God, we all must ageee, could not fall in this form of displeasure on His beloved Son. There can be no talk of placation or mollifying. And by the wrath of God we mean, and see that the Bible means, the judgment of a holy God upon sin even more than the disposition of God towards the sinner.

7. We can no longer separate Christ's life of obedience from His expiatory death. He was obedient, not simply *in* death, but *unto* death. But this means not a tuning down of His death, but a tuning up of His life. It means that His whole person was expiatory in its ultimate function and supreme work. It was on this ground that He forgave sin during His life. Each miracle cost, and was preceded by, a small Passion. His sorrowful existence was an expiation. All His sufferings were death in advance, deaths manifold, chastisements of sin, and in their nature expiatory. He was inwardly in deaths often before He died the outward death.

8. We are, I hope, all giving up the tendency to twist Scripture into support of our theories, orthodox or liberal. In particular, scholarship more and more unanimously compels us to give up the Roman idea that justifying in St. Paul means making just and not declaring just; or that "the righteous-

ness of God" means the ethical attribute of God conveyed to us, rather than the gift of God as a status conferred on us. On such points the old theology and the new exegesis unite. The finality of Paul's authority, of course, is a separate question, but his meaning should not be longer in dispute.

By justification Paul at least meant something more forensic than ethical, a fiat more than a verdict of God, something more creative than appreciative, more synthetic than analytic. It was most original and wonderful, a new morality more moral than any natural ethic, and high removed from the judgment of the natural traditional conscience.

9. We are leaving behind us, to all appearance, the hazy idea that we have the fact of the Atonement and that no theory need be sought or can be found. The fact of the Crucifixion does not depend on theory, but a fact like the Atonement can be separated from theory of some kind only by a suffusion of sentiment on the brain, some ethical anæmia, or a scepticism of the spiritual intelligence.

10. We are abandoning the idea that any adequate treatment of this great and solemn theme can rest on the basis of a merely personal experience. Amateur and dilettanti theologising, however devout, is, by its very individualism, disqualified for any very valuable verdict on such a universal theme. The history of the question in the Church is as little to be despised as it is to be idolised. If we fall back on experience the question is too vast for any single experience, and what we must use is the experience of the Church. Yet even that is not final. The Bible must still save us from the Church. And I hope we have outgrown the idea that anything so subjective as the Christian consciousness can be the test of truth which, in its very nature as a saving power, must be in the first place objective. Our forgiveness has an objective ground, and is inseparable from the death of Christ, and from that death considered as something more than the source of a new type of experience.

11. Expiation and forgiveness, it has been said, are mutually exclusive. If a sin has been

expiated the account is cleared; there is then no need of forgiveness or question of Grace. This was the criticism of Socinius on Anselm. May we hope that we are beyond that, that it is seen to miss the mark as soon as the quantitative and equivalent theory of Christ's suffering is given up? Of course, an expiatory *amount* of penalty purges the offence; and, the debt being paid, the culprit is beholden to no grace for his open door. But if we say that God, who had a right to destroy each sinner, offers pardon to those who really own in the Cross the kind (not the amount) of penalty which their sin deserved, then the contradiction vanishes. Grace is still sovereign, free and unbought. It is grace in God to accept an Atonement which is not an equivalent but a practical, adequate, and superhuman acknowledgment in man of the awful debt foregone.

II.—Positive.

12. We must go beyond even the texts bearing on this subject. The classic texts have for the present been well-nigh exhausted.

The separation of Biblical from dogmatic theology has left the Church free as it never was before to recognise where the value of texts ceases and to abstain from pressing them to their hurt. And I come now to the more positive part of my work when I say that we must start from the actual spiritual situation of our day, and begin with the ruling contemporary idea to which the Spirit has led us in His teaching and unteaching of His Church. That ruling idea is revelation. Jesus Christ makes the claim He does upon the world not as being a religious genius, but as being the Revelation of God. What, then, is involved in the way of Atonement or Expiation in the Christian revelation of the love of God; in God not simply as the Father, but as the Father *of our Lord and Saviour Jesus Christ and Him crucified?* I mean by the Christian Revelation the revelation that Christ effected, and not only what He taught. Is it a revelation of such love as includes in itself, in its own spiritual necessity, the judgment upon sin, and includes it not as a mere principle, but as an accomplished and exhibited moral fact? Have we a revelation of love which not only produces repentance by its effect upon man, but also includes within itself the actual judgment and destruction of sin; and includes it not as a necessity probable in human thought, but as an active constituent of the revelation? Is it possible to have any adequate sense of the actual love of God in Christ without an equally real sense of His actual condemnation of sin? —its condemnation *in act*, note, not its mere hatred; and its condemnation, not in our experience but in Christ's. Is revelation separable from judgment, as an actual element of it and not merely as a coming corollary? Can there be any assertion of *forgiving* love without an assertion, equally actual and adequate, of the moral majesty of that love, and its difference from mere kindness? Was the revelation of holy love not equally and at once, in the same fact, a revelation of sin, a developing of sin to its utmost crisis, and to its final judgment? "God is Love" has in the New Testament no meaning apart from the equally prominent idea of righteousness, of God as the author and guardian of the moral holy law. The Christian principle of pardon is not forgiveness to repentance (no strong man forgives a real wrong on a thin repentance, a mere attrition), but to due repentance. And a due repentance means a repentance not only sincere (and certainly not equivalent), but containing some adequate sense of the evil done. And that means an adequate recognition in experience of the majesty and inviolability of the law of holiness. But such a recognition is not possible to a sinful soul or race. It could only be made by a conscience unblunted in its moral perceptions because sinless in its moral obedience, yet identified in sympathy with the sinful race. It is this practical and experienced recognition that is the Atonement or Expiation. It is ratifying by act and experience, by assent which was response and by a response which was lived and died, God's death sentence on sin. It is not repentance in Christ's case, but it is the source of repentance in us who are joined with Him. And the two polar experiences, joined in one spiritual and organic act of mystic union, form the complete type of Christian faith. The repentance is ours alone; the penalty is not, the judgment is not. The penal judgment or consequence or curse of sin did fall on Christ, the penitential did not. The sting of guilt was never His, the cry on the cross was no wail of conscience. But the awful atmosphere of guilt *was* His. He entered it, and died of it. Our chastisement was on Him, but God never chastised Him. The penalty was His, the repentance remains ours. His expiation does not dispense with ours, but evokes and enables it. Our saving repentance is not due to our terror of the judgment to fall on us, but to our horror of the judgment we brought on Him. The due recognition of the wounded law was His, but the sense of having inflicted the wound is ours alone. Yet not possibly ours till we are acted on by what was His. The truth of penalty is penitence. The end and intent of the judgment on Him was our judgment of ourselves in

Him. The use of penalty is to rouse the true punishment in all penalty, viz., the sense of guilt and personal repentance. Repentance is never regarded in Christianity as a thing possible by itself, or a condition effectual by itself without God, but only as that part or action of the complete work of Christ which takes effect through us. It is the form assumed by the work of Christ, the judgment on Christ, as it enters our atmosphere of personal guilt.

The question really is, Where did the difficulty lie that was to be overcome by Redemption? Was it in forgiving the penitent, or in producing the penitence that could be forgiven? Was it in God or in man, in the Divine conscience or the human? Where did Christ feel that the obstacle lay with which He had to deal? Was the objective of the Cross our human impenitence or something superhuman? Did He close with something which had no right, or something which had every right, with human hostility or Divine claim? Was He dealing with a human attitude or with a Divine relation? Was He engrossed with what He was doing toward men or toward God?

If we select one of these ways of putting it and ask whether the difficulty lay in producing forgiveness or forgiveableness, we must answer that it was both. The antithesis is but on the surface. They unite below. That which really produces forgiveable penitence in man is the expiation to law which bore first on God. It was to the law that produces penitence that forgiving grace had to die. The moral effect of the Cross on man is due to a nature in man continuous with the moral nature of God.

Love's awful moving cost in satisfying the broken law and maintaining its holy and inviolable honour, is the only means of producing such a sense of guilt as God can forgive. The difficulty of true repenting is the difficulty of realising that God took the broken law of His holiness so much to heart that it entailed the obedience in agony and death of the Holy One. Without the death of Christ the sinner feels that he is pursued only by an unexhausted judgment; and the end of that may be panic, but not penitence. It is the exhaustion of judgment and not its remission that produces the penitence which is forgiveably sensible both of the goodness and the severity of God.

It is the impossibility of remitting judgment that makes possible the remission of sin. The holy law is not the creation of God but His nature, and it cannot be treated as less than inviolate and eternal, it cannot be denied or simply annulled unless He seem false to Himself. If a play on words* be permitted in such a connection, the self-denial of Christ was there because God could not deny Himself.

I repeat, the form in which the question presents itself to-day is whether Redemption is a constituent element of Revelation or only a consequence of it; and whether it is so, both in a theological analysis of the idea, and as an interpretation of the spiritual fact and act, Christ, in His historic totality.

We may mark these stages at which my space will only allow me to hint.

* I take shelter under Matt. xvi. 25.

(1) Redemption is a part of Revelation. Revelation is not Revelation till it is effectual, *i.e.*, till it come home as such. A revelation merely displayed is none. It is not revelation till it strike light on the soul. The very first revelation involved the creation of a man to receive it; Revelation and Creation were one act. So the second and greater Revelation was not mere illumination or mere impression. It was Redemption. It involved the recreation of the soul to take it in. Revealing was *ipso facto* remaking, as a great and original genius has slowly to create the taste to appreciate him. The act which reveals his soul makes his world. If only we could grasp the idea of revelation as something done instead of something shown, as creation instead of exhibition, as renovation instead of innovation, as resurrection instead of communication.

(2) Atonement is a constituent of Redemption. The thing we are to be redeemed from is not chiefly ignorance or pain, but guilt. The thing to which revelation has first to address itself is guilt. The love of God can

only be revealed to sinful men as in primary relation not to lovelessness but to guilt. It can only appear as atoning love in some form of judgment.

We are to be redeemed by judgment somewhere from condemnation, from the wrath of God. There is no question of placation, but there is of expiation, of owning the holiest law by the holiest sacrifice and the humblest grief. There is a question of that law which to recognise as co-eternal with love is *the* sign of religious earnestness and virility. Salvation must be salvation not *from* judgment, but *by* judgment. Christ did not simply pronounce jugment, but effected it. And He gave it effect in His own person and experience. He bore the infinite judgment He pronounced. The prophet of woe becomes in a few chapters the victim of woe (Matt. xxiv., xxv., xxvi.). The agent of judgment becomes the object of judgment, and so becomes the agent of salvation. As Judge of all the earth, as the Conscience of the conscience, Christ is absolute in His judgment, unsparing and final in His condemnation. But as the second Adam and Man of men He attracts, accepts and absorbs in Himself His own holy judgment; and He bears, in man and for man, the double crisis and agony of His own two-edged vision of purity and guilt. He whose purity has the sole right to judge has by the same purity the only power to feel and realise such judgment. And His love made that power for Him a duty. And so He was their Saviour.

(3) Need it be said that Atonement for us is as impossible by us as it is necessary to holiness? Amendment is not reparation; and repentance even cannot lift itself to the measure of the broken law or gauge how great the fault has been. If made, the reparation must be made by God Himself. The sacrifice flows from grace and does not produce grace. It is not a case of altering God's disposition but His relations with man, of enabling Him to treat man as He feels. It is persistently overlooked that it is an act of grace and not of debt on God's part to accept even the satisfaction and

atonement of Christ for human forgiveness. We must never use the word satisfaction, even of Christ's sacrifice, in any way which would suggest equivalence, and constitute mere claim on God, any more than mere exemption for us.

Atonement is substitutionary, else it is none. Let us not denounce or renounce such words, but interpret them. They came into existence to meet a spiritual necessity, and to sweep them away is spiritual wastefulness, to say no worse. We may replace the word substitution by representation or identification, but the thing remains. Christ not only represents God to man but man to God. Is it possible for any to represent man before Holy God without identifying himself in some guiltless way with human sin, without receiving in some way the judgment of sin? Could the second Adam be utterly untouched by the second death? Yet if the Sinless was judged it was not His own judgment He bore, but ours. It was not simply on our behalf, but in our stead—yet not quantitatively, but centrally. Representation apart from substitution implies a foregone consent and election by the represented, which is not Christ's relation to humanity at all. Let us only be careful that we do not so construe the idea as to treat the sufferings of Christ as in real parity with ours. That is a moral impossibility, and lands us, as has been said, in all the anomalies of an equivalent theology which it is the merit of Socinus to have destroyed. The principle of a vicarious Atonement is bound up with the very idea of Revelation, of love emerging into guilt. There is an atoning substitution and a penal; but a penitential there is not.

(4) I can only here say a closing word on this last distinction. I do not see why we should avoid describing the suffering of Christ as penal. Nor do I see how we can. Sin is punished by suffering. And it was because of the world's sin that Christ suffered. It was the punishment of sin that fell on Him. He came deliberately under that part of the moral order which we may call the Divine and universal Nemesis. Christ loved holiness at least as much as He loved man; and the willing

penalty of the Holy One was the only form in which wounded holiness could be honoured, and love be revealed as in earnest with sin. It was, moreover, the only way in which penalty or law could produce its fruit of repentance, and so of reconciliation. Expiation is the condition of reconciliation. Penalty, if not vicarious, if its source do not also suffer, only hardens and alienates. The suffering was penal in that it was due in the moral order to sin. It was penal to Christ's personality, to His consciousness, but not to His conscience. It was not penitential. There was no self-accusation in it. He never felt that God was punishing Him, though it was penalty, sin's Nemesis that He bore. It was the consequence of sin, though not of His sin. And it was the consequence attached *by God* to sin—sin's penalty; and He so recognised it. It was judgment, and therefore penalty, and not mere pain or trial. Suffering does not repair sin; only penalty does, working to repentance. But it was not substitutionary *punishment*. There is no such thing in the moral world. The worst punishment is to see the penalty we brought on Christ—whether we see it with faith in a saving way, or without faith to our deeper condemnation.

To the question what the worth was which God saw in the work of Christ, and what the delectation which gave it saving value to His eye of grace, the answer can here be but in useless brevity. First, the practical and adequate recognition of a broken law in a holy and universal life is an end in itself, and therefore a Divine satisfaction. Second, the effect of that vicarious and loving sacrifice on men must bring them to a repentance and reconciliation which was the one thing that God's gracious love required for restored communion and complete forgiveness. He could now deal with them as He had felt from before the foundation of the world. It satisfied the claim and harmony of His holy nature, and it satisfied the redemptive passion of His gracious heart. Thirdly, that effect on men is due to the satisfaction of God's moral nature in the constitution of man. God was in Christ reconciling the world by the sacrifice and satisfaction of Himself.

Human illustrations are more useful for impression than for explanation in a case so original and unique as Christ's, yet I may close with one less common than some.

Schamyl was the great religious and military leader of the Caucasus who for thirty years baffled the advance of Russia in that region, and, after the most adventurous of lives, died in 1871. At one time bribery and corruption had become so prevalent about him, that he was driven to severe measures, and he announced that in every case discovered the punishment would be one hundred lashes. Before long a culprit was discovered. It was his own mother. He shut himself up in his tent for two days without food or water, sunk in prayer. On the third day he gathered the people, and pale as a corpse, commanded the executioner to inflict the punishment, which was done. But at the fifth stroke he called "Halt!" had his mother removed, bared his own back, and ordered the official to lay on him the other ninety-five, with the severest threats if he did not give him the full weight of each blow.

This is a case where his penalty sanctified her punishment both to herself and to the awestruck people.

Every remission imperils the sanctity of law unless he who remits suffers something in the penalty foregone; and such atoning suffering is essential to the revelation of love which is to remain great, high and holy.

Finally, if the Cross be penal we have not only to *admit* that it is so, but to *urge* it; for it is of the essence of its value for the soul, and the real secret of the Church's action on the world.

IV.

BY LYMAN ABBOTT, D.D.

AGAMEMNON has taken as a prize in war Chryseis, the daughter of Chryses, the priest of Phœbus, and has refused to allow her father to ransom her. In consequence Phœbus has sent a pestilence into the Greek camp, and the people are perishing. To appease the angry god, Ulysses is sent to return the captured daughter to her father. Leading her to her father and bringing the fat beeves as a gift to the angry god, "the wise Ulysses" speaks thus:

> O Chryses! Agamemnon, King of men,
> Sends me in haste to bring this maid to thee
> And offer up this hallowed hecatomb
> To Phœbus, for the Greeks; that so the god
> Whose wrath afflicts us sore may be appeased.

The Apostle John, interpreting the sacrifice of Jesus Christ, says:

God so loved the world that He gave His only begotten Son, that whosoever believeth in Him should not perish, but have everlasting life.

These two quotations, one from Homer the

greatest of the Greek poets, the other from John, the beloved of the Twelve Apostles, interpret two contrasted conceptions of sacrifice. In these conceptions there is a threefold difference.

In the pagan conception God is wrathful; in the Christian conception God is Love.

In the pagan conception man is wise, usually wiser than the god whose stern mood he softens; in the Christian conception man is destroying himself by his ignorance and his sin.

In the pagan conception the sacrifice is offered by man to appease the wrath of the god; the peril comes from the god, the salvation from "wise Ulysses"; in the Christian conception the sacrifice is made by God to give life to man; the peril comes to man from himself, the salvation from God.

The history of sacrifice in the Jewish Church in the Old Testament is a history of the gradual process by which the pagan conception was transformed into the Christian conception. Nor will it seem strange to us that the process was a very gradual one, if we consider what moral as well as intellectual transformation was required. Before the Christian conception of sacrifice could supplant the pagan, it was necessary that man should have such a spiritual reverence for God as would lead him to be more susceptible to the love of God than to fear of His wrath; that he should have such humility as to regard himself never as the inspirer of God's mercy, but wholly as the subject of a mercy unpurchased and unpurchasable; and that he should have such a sense of *self*-sacrifice as would lead him to comprehend the sacrifice offered by the injured for the injurer, not by the injurer to the injured. The revolution in thought was so great that it has not yet been fully accomplished, and in much of modern theology there is an attempt to intermingle the pagan and the Christian conceptions of sacrifice; to conceive of God as angry; to conceive of man as by his repentance and acceptance of a vicarious sacrifice securing the Divine favour; to conceive of the sacrifice itself as offered by one Divine Person to appease the wrath and satisfy the justice or fulfil the law of another Divine Person. But in fact no conception of sacrifice corresponds with the teaching of the New Testament, with the life of Christ, or with the interpretation of that life by Paul, or, indeed, with the highest phases of Christian experience as expressed, not in volumes of theology, but in the most spiritual hymns of the Christian Church, which does not in these three respects embody the Christian conception and disregard or practically deny the pagan conception. In the Christian conception sacrifice is wholly an expression of Divine love; it is wholly *self*-sacrifice, and its object is to impart life by God the Life-giver to man the perishing.

There is not space in so brief an article as this must be to trace the Old Testament history of this transformation. In that history the pagan and the Christian conceptions are seen in conflict: the pagan is the popular one, and it is supported, as in all ages of the world it has been, by the hierarchy. It is most clearly seen in the Levitical code, though even there greatly modified from the earlier pagan forms. The Christian or spiritual conception underlies the prophetic teaching, and grows more and more clear as the nation grows in spiritual development, until in Isaiah it is almost as clearly enunciated as in Paul himself. That sacrifice proceeds from God to man, not from man to God, is implied even in the Levitical code. This is recognised by the most orthodox divines. Says Rev. Alfred Barry, B.D., in Smith's Bible Dictionary, "Whereas the heathen conceived of their gods as alienated in jealousy or anger, to be sought after, and to be appeased by the unaided action of man, sacrifice represents God Himself as approaching man, as pointing out and sanctioning the way by which the broken covenant should be restored."

It is made to appear also in the Levitical code, scarcely less clearly, that the value of the sacrifice is not in any imagined effect on God, but in its efficacy as an expression of the mind and heart of the worshipper. No importance is attached to the intrinsic value of the thing sacrificed; it may be a heifer, a pair of doves, a sheaf of wheat; human sacrifice is forbidden; great hecatombs are no longer offered; attempts to appease God by costly offerings are unknown; sacrifice is not compulsory, it must be a freewill offering; and in its three chief forms it represents, never an attempt to appease the Divine wrath or win the Divine favour, but an attempt to express a divinely inspired experience—penitence by the sin-offering, gratitude by the thank-offering, consecration by the burnt-offering. Yet still the prophets see a danger of recurrence to the pagan conception and constantly warn against it. So that it is not too much to say that the whole Old Testament teaching is summed up in the words of the fifty-first Psalm, " Thou desirest not sacrifice, else would I give it; thou delightest not in burnt-offering. The sacrifices of God are a broken spirit; a broken and a contrite heart, O God, Thou wilt not despise."

The third point in the Christian sacrifice, that it is *self*-sacrifice offered by God Himself for man, is not so clear. Yet it is hinted at even in the earliest teachings, as in the story miscalled in common parlance "The Sacrifice of Isaac," in which God intervenes to forbid the sacrifice of his son by Abraham, and Himself provides a sacrifice which Abraham may use as an expression of his gratitude and self-dedication; it is implied in the teachings of Hosea, whose mercy toward his apostate wife serves as a parable of the unbought mercy of God seeking to call back an apostate nation to life; and it is explicit in the teachings of the second Isaiah concerning the Suffering Servant of God who was "despised and rejected of men, a man of sorrows and acquainted with grief."

It would imply extraordinary self-conceit to attempt to furnish in an article what I would not venture to attempt in a treatise—a complete theory of the Atonement. But the three principles indicated above may be safely applied to any theory on which our judgment is asked.

I. No theory of the Atonement can be correct which represents it as a method of appeasing God's wrath, or satisfying His justice, or meeting the requirements of His law, or devised as a substitute for punishment due to infraction of that law. This is to substitute in what Luther called the "Little Gospel," quoted from John above, for the thought of God's love—"God so *loved* the world," the thought of His wrath or justice or law. The Atonement proceeds not from God's law or justice or wrath, but from His love. What makes it necessary is not the necessity of inflicting penalty on lawbreakers, or of satisfying justice, or of appeasing wrath; what makes it necessary is God's love, "the great love wherewith He loved us, even when we were dead in trespasses and sins." It was not man in Christ suffering on behalf of man who reconciled the world to God; it was God in Christ who reconciled the world to Himself.

II. No theory of the Atonement can be correct which implies, directly or indirectly, that it is offered by man or on behalf of man to God. Whether the sacrifice be a hecatomb offered by "wise Ulysses," or a bloodless sacrifice of the Mass offered by a Roman

Catholic priest, or an imitation of such Mass offered by an Anglican Catholic priest, or a demand that the worshipper by an act of faith make the sacrifice of Christ his own— if the sacrifice is conceived as offered by or on behalf of man to God, and its object to produce an effect on the mind and heart of God—it is so far pagan, not Christian. The Christian offering was conceived by God and proceeds from God. It is not without significance that Paul never says Christ died in the stead of man, but always on behalf of man, (never αντὶ anti, but always ὑπέρ huper). It is not without significance that John declares that God *sent* His Son to be the propitiation for our sins. The propitiation comes from the One to be propitiated; it is self-propitiation. The Atonement is the expression of Divine love for man, not the means of winning that love. "God commendeth His love toward us in that, while we were yet sinners, Christ died for us."

III. No theory of the Atonement, therefore, can be correct which represents the object of the Atonement to exert an influence by man upon God; it is, on the contrary, God's method of exerting an influence upon man. Let me not be misunderstood. Of all theories of the Atonement, that which represents the crucifixion of Christ as a dramatic spectacle, devised to produce an emotional effect upon a world of spectators, appears to me the least deserving of intellectual or spiritual effect. Let it once be understood that this sacrifice is part of a "plan of salvation" gotten up for emotional effect, and it will have no emotional effect; as the mother who sheds tears to influence her boy, simply disgusts him; and the preacher who affects tears in his preaching produces amusement in his auditors. But the object of the Atonement is not an appeal by, or on behalf of man to God for mercy; it is a free grant of mercy by God to man. Self-sacrifice is the Divine method of life-giving.

It costs something to the doctor to heal a patient; more for a scholar to teach an ignoramus; most of all for a holy soul to cleanse an unholy one and give life to one that is dead. An unsuffering patriot can do little for his country in a crisis; an unsuffering believer nothing for his church in the time of its moral peril; an unsuffering mother cannot recover a wayward child from his sins; and an unsuffering God could not redeem a perishing world. The passion of Christ tells the world what sin is, for it tells how a sinful world treats perfect love. It tells us what love is, for it tells us what the Divine love is willing to suffer for a sinful world. The object of the Atonement is not to enable man to escape penalty, it is to redeem him from sin. If the reader will take his Bible, and examine with care the passages most frequently quoted in support of the doctrine of the Atonement, he will find that not one of them connects sacrifice with the remission of penalty; they all connect it with deliverance from sin: "The Lord hath laid on Him the *iniquity* of us all"; "The blood of Jesus Christ His Son cleanseth us from *all sin*"—these two passages, one from the Gospel of Isaiah, the other from the Gospel of John, are typical of the teaching of both the Old and the New Testaments on this subject.

The doctrine of the Atonement which we hold logically carries with it a corresponding conception of forgiveness and sacrifice as between man and man. We are bidden to be imitators of God as dear children. What does this mean? If He never forgives without exacting a penalty, if it is necessary that some one should suffer vicariously for the sinner before God can pardon him, then we, too, as imitators of God, will demand, before we forgive him who has sinned against us, either that he suffer or that some one suffer in his stead. If God, that He may forgive, suffers, if He endures self-sacrifice in the person of His Son, that He may redeem from their own undoing those who have done Him wrong, then in imitation of His example and as participators in His love we shall gladly offer self-sacrifice, if by it we can redeem from self-inflicted penalty the one who has wronged us.

What, then, I have tried to say in this article, which I have purposely made simple, is all summed up in these three propositions: The object of the Atonement is the purification of man, not the appeasement of God; the Atonement is made by God, not by man, nor by any one acting for or in place of man; and the inspiration of the Atonement is the love of God, not His law, His justice or His wrath.

V.

BY ADOLF HARNACK, D.D.,
Professor of Church History in the University of Berlin.

The Christian religion revolves round two focal points—Holiness and Forgiveness. Its simplest expression is naturally the confession of Almighty God as the Father, but even this includes within it the obligation and the power to lead a holy life and the assurance of forgiveness.

Christianity is the religion of redemption because it is the religion of forgiveness. The petition, "Forgive us our trespasses," answers to the certain belief that God really forgives trespasses. In the forgiveness of sins the Christian recognises redemption. Luther, who in his "Smaller Catechism" wrote, "Wherever forgiveness of sins is, there also is life and blessedness," was not the first to declare this. It was the Lord Himself, who in that Gospel of His in outline—the parable of the Prodigal Son—showed how the right of the son to his father's house followed forgiveness. The newly-found son participates in all his father possesses ; in forgiveness he has found redemption.

If, however, one looks upon the Christianity of to-day, it would appear as though the belief in redemption had lost its certitude. There are thousands who hold to monotheism and the ethics of Christianity who will hear nothing of redemption. To such the idea of it has no actuality; it is merely an historical conception, or, at best, a cause of passing emotion. To bring the idea of redemption into connection with the person of Christ appears to them an impossibility. They think that they can satisfy themselves with a Christianity without redemption and without Christ. For the same reason they also set aside the Church's conception of Christianity, in which redemption through Christ is the cardinal doctrine. There are various grounds for this attitude. Some say they do not feel any necessity for redemption; others see in the doctrine something weak and feminine, at variance with serious, virile ethics; others, again, recognise indeed the necessity of redemption, but think that the teaching of the Church on this point is erroneous, and that a person who lived eighteen hundred years ago cannot possibly be a redeemer for to-day. They are all, however, more or less moved by the conviction that our modern knowledge of the world, of man and of history, does not permit us to retain the idea of redemption. Psychology has given us a new picture of man; the investigations regarding the origin of morality have altered our notions of sin; historical science has given us an historical Jesus in place of the ecclesiastical Christ; critical philosophy has drawn with firm lines the boundaries of the possible and the real—what room is there, therefore, for the conceptions of redemption and of a redeemer?

In reality, while modern knowledge has rudely shaken the *form* of the doctrine in which earlier generations laid down their belief in redemption and in the Redeemer, the thing itself has not been shaken. "Mankind is always progressing, but man remains always the same," says Goethe somewhere. This deliverance might seem pessimistic, but it has its noble side. Man does not remain the same only in that which is bad and low, but also in those higher necessities which soar above the world of the earthly. St. Augustine's saying, "Thou, Lord, hast made us for Thyself, and our heart is not at rest until it finds peace in Thee," will find a response in human hearts as long as mankind lives on this earth, nor will the message of redemption and of a Redeemer ever be lost. In what follows, certain points of view are set forth, in which it is attempted concisely to justify the Christian belief in redemption. My object is rather to bring facts to remembrance than to prove any particular position.

I. Those who profess to find in themselves no need for redemption either deceive themselves, or they are thinking of only one particular kind. The need is a universal one. I do not mean the common desire for the bettering of one's own position, but rather that deeper feeling—the wish to be freed from the life which surrounds us, and to win a new and higher existence. We have only to open our eyes to see hundreds of redeemers offering themselves and promising redemption to the eager multitudes who surround them. There are devilish redeemers like intoxication and wild voluptuousness. Redemption is promised by art and science to their votaries. There are those who put their trust in writers, poets and philosophers, and announce that they have found through them the way of redemption. The world is full of prophets and messiahs— they are, of course, no longer called so. But that which they will not let die, that which they always reawaken is a noble aspiring. Everywhere amongst men is the desire to soar above the stream of the commonplace; they will not remain for ever submerged in it and lost; they yearn ceaselessly for deliverance from their servitude into a nobler form of life.

II. But this longing after redemption may be more definitely described. Wherever the Christian religion has come, wherever the faintest beam of it has been kindled, the idea gains possession of the soul that righteousness is the highest good and that guilt is the deepest evil. To be pure and to possess inward peace, that is the longing of longings. Only speak the right word to a man, search out the way to his soul, and you will find that this longing has not yet died out—to possess good thoughts and a pure heart. It is not true that the majority of men are so sunk in the ordinary egoistical business of life as to have quite lost the feeling for that which is holy and pure, nor is it true that modern science has the power to extinguish this sense. If it be granted that the scientific movement has with many induced a somewhat lower view of the human inner life, yet it has not radically changed it. No matter how our moral sensibilities may have been acquired, even though it may be pointed out that we were once a higher order of beasts, even though it may be established that there is no such thing as absolute freedom, yet still we perceive that our responsibility towards good and evil is a sort of natural law, and no science can take away from us for long the nobility of this responsibility. What though we show the butterfly that at one time it could only crawl and not fly; that does not alter the fact that it is to-day no longer a caterpillar but a butterfly. Mankind has experienced a somewhat similar metamorphosis. When that mighty change began no one knows. Its origin lies beyond the range of history. But its results are gloriously in view in the time of the Hebrew prophets and of Socrates and Plato. Still more clearly was it manifested to the whole Helleno-Roman world by Jesus Christ and His disciples. Regarded from the outside, history seems to have altered little; it is still filled with war and bloodshed, with the conflict for worldly possessions. And yet there was something new. Goethe remarked it, and the penetrating eye of the historian confirms the fact. The real theme of history for nearly two thousand years has been the struggle between belief and unbelief, the battle for God and for redemption. Mankind is wrestling, aided by the powers of the moral and holy, to be freed from the service of transitory things. There are some modern writers of history who would persuade us that this is an illusion, and that the theme of the world's history is still the struggle to possess that which is of the earth earthy. They are mistaken. If it were necessary there are thousands and thousands who would relinquish all their earthly possessions, who for the sake of an ideal, even of an erroneous ideal, would part with life itself. They know of a higher existence than that of sensual life, and they struggle towards it.

III. If this be true, we have at once the conception of "Redemption." In the highest sense redemption can only be the power which helps us to a holy, pure life, and strengthens the conviction within us that the boon is not a mere variety of earthly existence, but a new and abiding life. There can be, moreover, no redemption for us which is consummated outside our spirit. The greatest events may have been accomplished on earth, or between earth and heaven, but these cannot afford us assistance so long as they have no relation to that which we ourselves experience. And when the question is of the power and certainty of a holy and abiding life, and there is the knowledge that mere worldly possessions can effect nothing towards this life, it is impossible to believe that redemption and the Redeemer can spring from that which is earthly. It follows, therefore, that only God Himself can be the Redeemer. The prophets and the singers of the Psalms knew this; they did not look to a human redeemer, but to God. "Whom have I in heaven but Thee? And there is none upon earth that I desire beside Thee. My flesh and my heart faileth, but God is the strength of my heart and my portion for ever." There has never been, down to our own day, any other experience amongst those who have sought after real redemption. They have sought God and have besought Him to grant them a pure heart and a right spirit. They have prayed that God might forgive them their trespasses and find entrance to their hearts.

IV. It would seem from this as though a

human redeemer were impossible. It does not only *seem* so; it *is* so. *God only is the Redeemer.* A mysterious bond unites each man with God, and it is only when he feels this personal bond and enters into inward intercourse with God that he can be redeemed. And yet Christendom calls Jesus Christ its Redeemer. How is this contradiction to be got rid of?

There are people whose religious predisposition is so powerful that they are able, without help, to find God and to live in Him; but the history of religion shows that such persons are rare, and that the great majority of our race has no part in their experience. The prophets beheld God, heard Him, felt His presence, and in these experiences they had the most certain knowledge of His existence. Religious history also demonstrates that such persons have a great task to perform for others —they proclaim God to their fellows, and strengthen their weak consciousness of God. In most human beings this consciousness is not so strong that it can exist without this help. As in the case of Art, so here. We have all a certain predisposition for art, but it is only with the help of the artists that this predisposition is strengthened. One artist kindles the other, and one prophet anoints the other. We have here historical adjustment and an historical chain. Full independence, liberty and power are always the result of dependence and education.

It was the greatest event in the history of religion when God was no longer sought in the beams of the sun, in tempests, in magical contrivances, but in the proclamations of holy men like the prophets. It was only then that religion became a part of the inward life united with morality. Mankind did not unlearn the awe with which they regarded the government of God in creation, but they looked to the prophets with a higher kind of awe, for in their spirit and word the Divinity was revealed. Mankind now learned that only in man could the highest and truest revelation of God be revealed, for God is the Holy One, and holiness cannot reveal itself in Nature. This was why the prophets were honoured, and why so unique a position was conceded to them. It was felt that without them mankind would have remained stationary in the ancient bondage. By believing in and following the prophets, that which they had experienced was taken hold of by the souls of men. In this sense they were redeemers, that is to say, messengers and mediators. It was not their own fire which they used to inflame souls, but they were the torches. The hearer who could not be certain of God by his own original religious individuality was enabled to apprehend Him by following the prophet, who drew him into the Divine fellowship.

V. Jesus Christ was a prophet. One must begin with this conception of His person and work. He who is incapable of comprehending the prophets and their mission in history cannot comprehend Jesus Christ. Christendom, however, does not only call Him a prophet, but distinguishes Him from all other prophets, and asserts that He is "the Redeemer." How is this assertion to be vindicated?

The simplest way seems to be to refer

to Christ's own evidence regarding Himself. There can be no doubt that He distinguished between Himself and the prophets, claiming for Himself an altogether peculiar position. But to maintain this would not help us if we could not at the same time perceive the justice of His claim. Blind acquiescence has no moral worth.

Jesus Christ was a prophet, but He was the last prophet. Those who came after Him were either false prophets, or they have confessed that they have drawn their grace from His abundance. And therefore we are no longer justified in calling those great men of God who succeeded Him prophets—Paul, John, Augustine, Francis, Luther and the rest. Jesus Christ was a prophet, but while the other prophets drew only small circles around them, He has become the prophet for the entire human race. Jesus Christ was a prophet, but while the earlier prophets possessed only an imperfect knowledge of God, one of them correcting the other, He has given the fullest revelation of God in His proclamation of God as the Father. Jesus Christ was a prophet, but while the life and calling of the earlier prophets were at variance, the sharpest eye could detect no difference between what He practised and what He preached. The Word of God His Father was His meat and drink. These are historical facts, and because of these facts it is our right and our sacred duty to regard Jesus Christ not as a prophet like the others. We must raise Him above their number, rendering Him special gratitude, and honouring Him with special reverence. He called Himself "the Son of God," and we understand that He was entitled to call Himself this. He led His disciples to the Father, and to-day His Gospel still leads men from the bondage of transitory affairs to the glorious liberty of the children of God. He promotes us to inward communion with God who redeems us.

VI. But that is not all. We do not think of censuring or of refusing the title of Christians to those who go no further than this. The apostolic announcement has, however, a much wider signification. First, in it Jesus Christ is called the Reconciler. It teaches that He died for sin. Secondly, it affirms that Jesus Christ dwells in the faithful, fills them, guides and governs them. "It is not I who live, but Christ which liveth in me."

I shall not dwell here upon the second point —viz., that He who has become our prophet, guide, and master, takes inward possession of us. It is not a paradox, it is a fact. But that which lies behind this fact, that which is expressed in the confession "Christ lives in me," the conviction, namely, of the eternal life of Christ, the power and the glory of it—this is a secret of faith which is not capable of demonstration. The first point, however, demands closer consideration. Christ died for our sins? Christ has reconciled God? How? Did God require a reconciliation? Is God not Love? Does the God who forgives sins, the God of mercy, require an indemnity? Did the Father in the parable of the lost son demand expiation before he forgave his son? Was it not said of him who prayed, "God be merciful to me a sinner," "This man went down to his house justified?"

Yes, it is certainly so. God is Love. He has always been Love, and will remain so. The consolation of the Gospel of Jesus consists, indeed, in this—that He has revealed unto us God as eternal Love. Far be the thought from us that God has been turned from wrath to love, and that something had to be paid or sacrificed in order that He might love and forgive. But with this acknowledgment the matter is not exhausted.

For there is an inner law that compels the sinner to look upon God as a wrathful judge. It is this conception of God which is the hardest and the most real punishment inflicted on sin. It tears the heart of man, transforms his thoughts of God into terror, robs him of peace and drives him to despair. This conception of God is a false one, and yet not false, for it is the necessary consequence of man's sin— that is to say, of his godlessness. How can this conception of God be overcome? Not by words, but by deeds. When the Holy One descends to sinners, when He lives with them and walks with them, when He does not count them as unworthy, but calls them His brethren, when He serves them and dies for them, then their terror of the awful judge melts away, and they believe that the Holy One is Love, and that *there is something mightier still than Justice —Mercy*.

It is in relation to these human conceptions that we have specially to regard the death of Christ. His death is thus the culminating point of the service which He rendered for sinners during His mission. This service had the single object of convincing sinners that forgiving Love is mightier than the Justice before which they tremble. If they believe this they are reconciled, and in this manner is the God of punitive justice reconciled. They now know God as their Redeemer, but they also know Jesus Christ as their Reconciler.

This is the fundamental form of the Christian belief of the atonement. I would avoid alleging that every Christian must think so. But this I know, that Jesus Christ has not called the righteous to Himself, but those who trembled before Righteousness, and that the deepest and most earnest Christians embrace Jesus Christ, not only as the Prophet, but as the Reconciler. They do not, however, rest satisfied with seeing the atonement only in the life-work of Christ. They consider also His passion and His death as vicarious. How can they do otherwise? If they, the sinners, have escaped justice, and He, the Holy One, has suffered death, why shall they not acknowledge that that which He has suffered was what they should have suffered? In presence of the Cross no other feeling, no other note, is possible. And for this reason it is little use speculating on the "saving value" of Christ's sufferings. To begin, in this region, to cast up reckonings is to lose the whole sacred impression of this divine fact upon the soul. Let us rather, with reverential reticence, gaze upon the Cross of Christ from which God shines forth as the Infinite Love. It is a holy secret not understood of the profane, and yet "the power of God and the wisdom of God"!

VI.

BY R. F. HORTON, M.A., D.D.,
Formerly Fellow of New College, Oxford.

"CHRIST died for our sins according to the Scriptures." That sentence sums up the whole Bible. The four Gospels teach us that Christ died, and the rest of the New Testament that He died for our sins. And the Scriptures— *i.e.*, the Old Testament—were in some mysterious fashion, by type, by allegory, by ethical and spiritual teaching, designed to prepare the human race for the truth which in the New Testament was revealed, that Christ died for our sins. If, therefore, by the word Atonement we understand, as is usually understood, the death of Christ for our sins, there is one decisive argument against the omission to preach it. The preacher in that case has to shut his eyes to the most decisive factor which gives unity to the whole Bible; he has to deliberately overlook, or to ingeniously explain away, not only a few texts, which may be easy, but the vertebral backbone of the Bible,

which is his authority for preaching and the
commission that he is to preach. This is a
very serious matter. Small wonder that a
Christian minister, who from intellectual difficulties, or from lack of spiritual experience,
ignores the Atonement, becomes either nerveless
and ineffectual or eccentric and sensational. His
message is gone; he is an ambassador without
his credentials. Consequently he either loses
heart and becomes altogether dull, or, if he is
a man of ability, he strikes out and endeavours,
by his own study or ingenuity or speculation, to
supply the gap which is made. But from the
nature of the case his ministry must cease to be
fruitful. He may, by the omission of the great
mystery, smooth down the difficulties of theological thought, and so give a temporary rest to
distracted minds. He may, by ethical discussions, by social reforms, by historical subjects,
and even by the recasting of theological
formulæ, awaken a keen interest and draw a
large congregation. But if by fruit is understood the conversion of souls, the changing of
bad men into good, inroads into the vast un-

christly world, and extension of the Kingdom through the world, it will be found that his ministry is no longer fruitful.

It was from a deep conviction that the Gospel is essentially the preaching of an Atonement, and yet from a feeling that no thinker had succeeded in giving a satisfactory *rationale* of the Atonement, that, six years ago, in that little-noticed book, "Faith and Criticism," I argued that the fact of the Atonement may reasonably be believed and made the subject of preaching, even though we are admittedly unable to give any thorough explanation of it. I write again on the subject now because I am bound to advance a little beyond the position then taken. I feel myself convinced by the argument of Rev. John Scott Lidgett, in his Fernley Lecture, "The Spiritual Principle of the Atonement." It would be presumptuous of me to give an estimate of the book. To praise it would be an impertinence; but I may at least say that it has moved me forward from the position which I defended in "Faith and Criticism," and I trust it may move forward any readers who were encouraged by my essay to remain in that provisional position. It seems to me that Mr. Lidgett makes out a strong case on two points. He shows that we may hope to arrive at the theory, or at least the Spiritual Principle, of the Atonement, and that the warring theories which have been suggested may be regarded as contributions from different sides, which in their totality may bring us to a complete and final view. This is an original mode of treatment which meets many of the difficulties which I felt six years ago. For instance, I purposely abstained from advancing my own theory of the Atonement, because I regarded the whole field of inquiry as strewn with the shreds of shattered systems. "True," says Mr. Lidgett in effect, "the field is strewn with the shreds of shattered theories; out of these shreds we may hope to construct the true theory." But the other point, which is even of more importance, is this: Mr. Lidgett has for the first time made clear to my mind the vital truth that the principle of the Atonement must be spiritual. For example, in discussing the interpretation which the Psalmists and Prophets put on the sacrificial system of the Law Mr. Lidgett says: "To sum up: The testimony of the Prophets and the Psalmists demands that the principle of the Atonement shall be truly spiritual, and shall stand in vital relation to the spiritual and ethical condition of those for whom it is effected. Suffering unconnected with conduct, even though the sufferer be Divine, vicarious sacrifice, if unrelated to the spiritual life of those for whom it is offered, would be out of harmony with all the principles which they have laid down."

Let me insist on this last point for a moment before reverting to the first. The Atonement must be spiritual. It must be a transaction in the realm of spirit, which, however it may be manifested in a visible act or suffering, is essentially in another sphere. While we lay the stress on a certain empirical event, a crucifixion, a shedding of blood, a *quid pro quo* we are regarding it still in the light of the blood of bulls and rams, those carnal ordinances which can never take away sins. But when we follow the work of Psalmists and Prophets, in getting at the spiritual principle which underlay the material sacrifices, we are obliged, with the writer to the *Hebrews*, to treat the sacrifice of Christ in the same way. Through the eternal Spirit He offered Himself. The cross, the spear, the nails, the crown of thorns are details, accidents of the situation. There can be no qualitative relation between such things and the forgiveness of sins. But that inward and spiritual transaction, that vast drama that was enacted in the spirit of Christ, of which we gain sufficient though momentary glimpses in His utterances on the cross, may easily be a deed of such quality and moment that it touches the whole body of human sin (which also is spiritual), and potentially, at any rate, bears it away. Evidently a spiritual transaction, which is not in space or time, is incommensurate with things which are in space and time. A spiritual transaction, which is not of the size or weight of a hair, a mere word or thought, may overbalance, and outweigh, the whole material universe. Illustration is difficult, and may only divert us from the thought. But suppose we grasp the truth that by the Word of God the heavens were made—that is to say, that by a spiritual energy expressed in a brief fiat the cosmic order came into existence—then we may faintly apprehend that by a brief spiritual utterance like the agony of the cross, a mystery of psychological acting and suffering into which the angels desire to look, the sins of the world were forgiven and taken away. I am conscious that in pressing this thought we find relief from many of the troubles which have beset our doctrine of Atonement. Why should it be thought a thing incredible that in a three hours' agony of the spirit of such an one as Jesus something should have been effected which would apply to all time, even retrospectively, to all the human race with which He was connected, to the whole creation in which it took place? It is the fixed habit of ignoring the *spiritual*, and materialising our religious ideas that has occasioned the difficulty; just the habit against which the Psalmists and Prophets protested—the habit of regarding the hecatombs of the Temple altar as in some way a substitute for the sacrifices of a contrite and believing heart. Just the same habit drove the unthinking materialism of the Catholic Church to lay increasing stress on the bloody sufferings of the cross, to exaggerate the physical horrors of the crown of thorns, the scourging and the nails, until no attention was paid to the movement within the soul of the Sufferer, the cup which He was deliberately drinking, the spiritual sacrifice which He was offering, the eternal victory which He was winning.

And before passing from this point we may observe that the spiritual principle of this Atonement turns on these two factors—first, the solidarity of Christ with the human race, which enabled Him to offer in His person what was, in idea, an offering of the Race; and second, the offering being that of obedience to the will of God, an utter, undeviating obedience, as we should put it, even unto death. These factors are, of course, not brought out by Mr. Lidgett for the first time; but they are brought out with peculiar force in connection with his central idea. Thus, while we are considering the sacrifice as carnal or physical, the solidarity of the human race does not help us, because we are not connected by physical nerves with our fellow-men; our physical pains are borne necessarily alone. But when we conceive the offering as in the spirit, the spiritual solidarity of the race becomes an illuminating idea, for it is not difficult to conceive how every spiritual struggle, pain, achievement, of every human being affects all the rest, to remotest generations. The spiritual nerves do run through all the spiritual organism of humanity. And so, that thought which is made prominent in the New Testament, that the offering of our Lord was one of obedience, taken in connection with the spiritual solidarity of the race, becomes intellectually satisfying, in proportion as we realise that it is man's disobedience which constitutes the Fall, and an alienation of heart that perpetuates it. Where the representative man, as the linked member of the whole human family, offers up a perfect obedience to God, there we can well understand that the breach between man and God is, at least potentially, healed.

And as we dwell upon the nature, the significance, the wide ramifications, of this central spiritual offering, in the person of Christ, we can see that such a transaction, and, indeed, that particular transaction and no other, was indispensable to the Divine pardon of sin and the salvation of the world.

But to revert to the first point, which makes the distinctive value of Mr. Lidgett's treatment. Instead of regarding the theories of Atonement which began with Anselm, and which, for the present, end with Ritschl, as conflicting and mutually exclusive, he sees in each one a definite contribution to a complete account of the "Spiritual Principle of the Atonement." Without going so far as to say that this complete account can now be given, he certainly feels that the contributions of the great thinkers all have their assigned place. The period of the general Councils, roughly speaking, succeeded, nine centuries after Christ, in defining the Person of Christ and His relation to the Godhead. As the nine centuries since Anselm draw to an end, the Church may succeed in defining the nature and doctrine of the Atonement. A few words may make plain in what way the Ecumenical Council of the Centuries has been in silent conclave on the matter working out the true doctrine of Atonement. The first great thinker on the subject, Anselm, in the *Cur Deus Homo*, established once for all the notion that God Himself was concerned, in order to perfect His work in creation, to deal with sin. He showed also how man could not of himself make a satisfaction for sin, or get rid of it without weakening the sense of it. This was the main thought contributed before the Reformation. Calvinism added the notion that our Lord's life was a necessary preparation for His atoning sacrifice, that we are in abiding relationship with Him, and His incarnation brought Him into the experience of the consequences of sin. To this Grotius contributed the thought that by the sacrifice of Christ the moral government of the universe was vindicated, and the Divine judgment on sin was expressed. In modern times Dr. Dale has the credit of bringing out the conception of righteousness as something quite distinct from the arbitrary will even of God, and the further credit of showing that God must mark the ill-desert of sin by suffering, so that the sufferings of Christ are a necessary element in Atonement. Dr. McLeod Campbell laid a strong stress on the spiritual nature of the Atonement, and on the need of entering into the mind of God concerning sin. Maurice added the notion that the Lord fulfils the true life of humanity, and becomes the root of a sinless humanity. In Bishop Westcott there is a contributory touch, that it was part of the Lord's work to be made perfect through suffering, which evolved His highest capabilities. Bushnell brought out the connection between Love and Sacrifice, and showed how Christ entered into the curse. Finally, Ritschl has insisted on the vital bond of love between God and man, and on the truth that the essence of Atonement is in ethical relations.

Thus, the great truth has been brought out in the process of the ages. And if the master-mind which can gather up all the strands of truth and twist them into one cord has not yet appeared, we may be thankful for the mind that has shown us these strands in the process perhaps of combination. We need not despair of understanding the nature of the Atonement, and so gaining power and freshness in our preaching of the fact. And though it be true that it is the fact and not the explanation of it that saves, and we should and must proclaim the Divine fact, even when our explanations are unsatisfactory even to ourselves, yet we are all aware that the proclamation of the fact will come with a force as of new revelation this age when preachers have obtained a satisfying *rationale* of it, and when

> Heart and mind agreeing well,
> Shall make one music as before.

VII.

BY WALTER F. ADENEY, M.A.,

Professor of New Testament Exegesis, History and Criticism, New College, London.

PERPLEXED by the theses of the schools and tired of interminable discussions, many people are settling down to the conclusion that, while they accept the fact of the Atonement, they must abandon all hope of arriving at any theory concerning it. The high authority of the late Dr. Dale is pleaded in defence of this separation of fact and theory, although that great theologian was not content to rest in any half-way house himself, and proceeded to work out a most elaborate argument in the region of hypothesis. I venture to say that the popular position is little better than a refuge for intellectual indolence, and cannot be taken as a final settlement of the momentous question with which it is concerned. At best it is but a provisional halting-place between the decaying systems of the past and the ideas that must be faced in the days to come, if religion is to have that grip on the mind which unthinking pietism can never attain to. We have to be on our guard against the illusions of language. The word "fact" has a tempting sound for the Englishman of Philistine proclivities. But what does it mean in that region where the spiritual work of our Lord Jesus Christ in reconciling souls with God is carried on? We need not confine it to what is visible or tangible, to mere matters of sense perception; inward experiences such as joy, love, hope, fear, are also legitimately reckoned facts. But here we are concerned with a region above and beyond all experience. The life and death of the Saviour we take to be facts; the recovery of men and women from lives of shame and folly as far as this can be observed may also be set down in the category of facts. But the connection between these two series traverses a vast expanse of theory. At all events, when we are discussing this connection we are moving in that borderland of ideas where fact passes over insensibly into theory. Here a well-established truth is counted a fact, while one less clearly determined goes into the category of theory, so that one man's fact may be but theory to another man. Is not this the case with regard to the Atonement, which, while it is solid fact to some of us, is reckoned by not a few people to belong wholly to the realm of speculation? Indeed, it is very difficult to say what we mean by the fact of the Atonement if we leave everything of a theoretical nature out of account.

But another objection must be raised to this easy popular solution of a theological difficulty by accepting the fact and disregarding the theory. In course of time the fact that is treated in this way, isolated from thought, detached from any system of related facts, unexplained and unjustified, must gradually fade out of consideration and sink into neglect, leaving the bare affirmation of it, if that is still repeated, as no better than the statement of a dead dogma. Custom and tradition may keep it with us for a little while, but only as a relic of antiquity, and it will surely wither and perish of intellectual starvation. Every truth that permanently affects the mind and heart, even though it be encircled with mysteries and beset with difficulties, must link itself on to our general conception of the universe, must in some way satisfy intellect and conscience. If our belief in the Atonement cannot do this, that belief is doomed, and the doctrine, as far as it is specific in its connection with the Cross of Christ, will have to be lopped off the tree of fruitful beliefs as a useless dead branch.

To judge by the silence of some preachers on the subject, it would appear that as far as they are concerned this result has already been attained. We have only to compare the prominence given to the doctrine of the Atonement in the sermons of the earlier evangelicals with the meagre references to it in much modern preaching by men who are willing to declare that they accept the fact without attempting any theory, to see that this admission of the fact amounts to very little. But there are some of us to whom it seems that such a result can be nothing less than a disaster. The history of the Church shows that in all ages the winning power of the Gospel has gone with a passionate preaching of redemption through the

Cross of Christ. The Fatherhood of God, the Brotherhood of Jesus, the ethics of the Sermon on the Mount, our Lord's magnificent conception of the kingdom of heaven—great truths that have come to the front in our own day, and for the clearer vision of which we may well be thankful—have none of them evinced the missionary energy, the evangelising efficacy, that have been found to accompany the preaching of salvation through the Cross. We are told to look to facts. This is a fact, the significance of which cannot be gainsaid. But now we must go a step further. Wherever this preaching of redemption through the crucified Christ has gone forth with the pathos and the passion without which it is not effective, it has been accompanied by what must be designated a theory of the Atonement, often crude, narrow, illogical, not seldom revolting and preposterous to the calm, critical mind of a later age, but still at the time intellectually satisfying. The awakened soul is not found to be brought into the new life by the bare presentation of the fact that somehow, we do not know how, the death of Christ secures his forgiveness. He in some way sees, or thinks he sees, the chasm cleft by his sin between him and God bridged over, by either the appeasing of the Divine wrath, or the satisfying of justice, or the settlement of legal claims, or some other definite process. We may object to each and all of these conceptions; we cannot deny that such have been the invariable accompaniments of fruitful evangelisation. If we hold they were errors, illusions, excrescences, accompanying but not assisting the course of events, we must give up our appeal to experience as a testimony to the importance of the Atonement. What, then, remains? The testimony of Scripture. Here is a truth repeatedly appearing in the Bible from Isaiah liii. to 1 John and the Revelation. But considering the present-day ideas on the subject of inspiration, and in view of modern methods of critical study, does anybody suppose that a profoundly mysterious doctrine, which is neither intellectually appropriated nor confirmed by experience, will hold its ground as an important truth of religion simply on the authority of textual assertions?

There is quite another consideration that rises up to rebuke the current indolent treatment of the subject. If it be in any sense true that Jesus Christ died on the cross for our sakes, the transcendent importance of such an action in our personal relations with our Lord Himself, the sense of gratitude, of love, of boundless devotion it should call forth, ought to outweigh all other thoughts and feelings, and fill our heavens from zenith to horizon. Such a truth, if it be a truth at all, is *the* truth of life and religion; it is as ungrateful as it is unreasonable to relegate it to a secondary place, rarely alluding to it, and then only in frigid generalities out of deference to an accepted creed from which the interest has evaporated.

It is necessary, then, on more accounts than one, that we should gird ourselves to the difficult task of grasping this great truth which we designate by the name "Atonement." And in doing so it will be important to guard against the danger of being led off on side-issues. One of the weightiest recent pronouncements on the subject is to be seen in Archdeacon Wilson's *Hulsean Lectures* on "The Gospel of the Atonement," the author of which shows the real importance of that factor in the life of the present day; and yet he does so by dwelling on its influence upon us in bringing us back to right relations with God. Now the truth and value of this influence cannot be denied; and yet experience shows that it is most powerfully felt when it is based on a belief in another aspect of the Atonement, a belief that Christ has done something for us in the direction of God, and what is called the *subjective* effect of the Atonement is found to be most pronounced just in proportion as there is faith in its previous *objective* efficacy. It is contrary to experience to suppose that the former can be maintained in its old vigour after the latter has been allowed to drop out of notice, or even to be repudiated as unreal. The one serious question concerning the whole subject lies here as to whether there is any *objective* element in it, and, if so, what that *objective* element is.

Now it is quite clear that the critical work of the earlier part of this century was most potent and final, especially when it was based on moral and spiritual grounds, as in the case of McLeod Campbell. Each conception of the Atonement that has held possession of the mind of the Church at successive epochs has interpreted itself in harmony with the ruling ideas of the age. Thus the grotesque patristic notion of a bargain with the devil corresponded to the demonology that played so large a part in early Christian thought; Anselm's discussion about the satisfaction of the personal rights of God as the Suzerain Lord of the Universe rested on the feudal conception of government that was flourishing in his day; the Protestant theology with its conception of law, and the claims of justice which must be satisfied, or of the debt that must be paid, if not by the debtor, then by some one else, harmonised with the rise of international law in the writings of Grotius, and the substitution of respect for law for the assertion of personal rights, which was one of the greatest changes marking the transition from mediæval to modern methods of government; while the commercial aspect of the doctrine synchronised with the great extension of trade that was seen in Europe during the sixteenth century. But with the abandonment of the old demonology, the decay of feudalism, the reluctance to admit the abstract claims of law as such, the feeling that religion must be regarded spiritually and not as a business affair, every one of these theories is swept away and cast into the limbo of dead beliefs. Or, if here and there a champion is found for one or other of them, we feel that his argument is purely academic. It is impossible for him to link it on to the living ideas that now flourish in our minds or awaken a sympathetic response among thinking people. Of course it is not to be denied that the most crude conceptions of the Atonement still linger on and assert themselves with considerable vehemence in circles of life that are untouched by movements of thought. They still dominate an eager, elementary evangelism. But the fact that there is this simple, unthinking earnestness among men and women who are doing a great practical work lays all the greater obligation on that part of the Church of Christ which is brought to a more intellectual grasp of ideas to set them out in a fashion that is conceivable to thinking people, for we must not forget that even thinking people have souls to be considered.

It may seem that we are called in this matter to the task of Sisyphus. Will the hill-top of absolute truth ever be attained? Perhaps not; but meanwhile every attempt to reach it brings out some phase or some relative truth that is of value by the way. Moreover, just in proportion as we are now trying to shake ourselves free from prejudices, and to apply for the first time in the history of religion the same unfettered methods of inquiry to religion that we are accustomed to employ in other regions of inquiry, there is some hope that we may not go egregiously wide of the mark. In particular, since historical exegesis is bringing out the genuine meaning of Scripture with an accuracy that was not attainable under earlier methods, it is easier for us than it was for people in any other age to understand what the Scriptures teach on the subject of the Atonement, and to trace the development of that teaching through the Old Testament and the New, dividing out the several ideas concerning it as they appear in prophets and apostles, as they are seen in Isaiah, or Paul, or John.

It is in accordance with the results of this exegesis that any intelligent conception of the Atonement is likely to be reached, at all events, by those who are willing to look for guidance in these teachers.

I fear I have already exceeded my limits. It would be vain for me to attempt to set forth the actual lines on which the theory of the Atonement may be worked out in our own days. But in concluding I may, perhaps, indicate what appears to me to be the direction in which our thoughts on this subject may be led. We can tolerate no theory that limits the freedom of

God's forgiveness, or fails to recognise that our redemption springs from His Fatherly love; no theory that juggles with truth in the name of justice, calling white black that it may call black white; and, on the other hand, no theory that treats sin lightly and the awful severance it creates between the soul and God as of little account. Wherever the sense of guilt is deep and agonising, conscience cries out for some effectual atonement. Now, is it not very significant that both St. Paul, in his weighty words recorded in the second chapter of the Epistle to the Philippians, and the author of the Epistle to the Hebrews, in his elaborate discussion of the cleansing effect of the death of Christ, where he repudiates sacrifices and offerings as of no value, lay stress on the obedience of Christ consummated in death—His being obedient unto death—as of supreme value in the sight of God? The sacrificial imagery may fall off as a mere form of Jewish thought, but the essential idea of the surrender of the will must remain as the heart and essence of all religion. That Christ faced death when it came in His way rather than desert His task is plainly a proof, we may say the crowning proof, of His absolute submission to His Father. And if it be asked, How can this perfect obedience of Christ be of any advantage to us? we have at least the analogy of intercessory prayer. Why should a mother pray for her son except that the devotion of one soul may bring blessing to a kindred soul? But St. Paul goes further in profound mysticism, teaching that faith in Christ is union with Christ, and never dissociating the work of Christ for us from the life of Christ in us.

VIII.

BY THE HON. W. H. FREMANTLE, D.D.,
Dean of Ripon.

THE great convictions which form the basis of our Christian life, though in essence they remain the same, yet change in their aspect and their enunciation; like some grand mountain, which, as we see it from different points of view, appears now as a pyramid, now as square-topped, sloping or precipitous, a mass or a cluster. And, when such a change of aspect is put into words, it usually begets controversy, which, however, undergoes the healing influence of time: the sides of the volcano are clothed with verdure after a few years.

Some forty years ago the doctrine of the Atonement was the subject of such a controversy. The views expressed by Frederic Maurice, by Professor Jowett, by McLeod Campbell, by Baldwin Brown and many others, startled the Christian mind, and were met by vehement reassertions of the old ideas, often in a crude and repulsive form. A whole volume of University sermons by men so different as Dr. Pusey and Bishop Baring was published at Oxford in 1856 "in reference to the views published by Mr. Jowett and others." But time has softened these asperities, and we can reason more calmly. Mutual confidence grows, and we find that criticisms and negations did not mean all that was supposed. On the question of the nature of the Atonement we may put aside many of the explanations given in past times, yet preserve a fast hold on Redemption through the death of Christ. Such representations as Athanasius's that the corruption of humanity through sin was done away by the death of Christ, since all died in Him (not in the moral sense of 2 Cor. v., but by physical death); or that of Origen that the devil's claims on mankind were paid off by the crucifixion; or that of Anselm that the sacrifice was by its excess of righteousness a satisfaction or making up for the defects of sinful men; or the later theory that Christ was punished instead of men, and that, because

He was punished, sinners are pardoned or "let off," cannot but seem to us either puerile or insufficient, even if they are not denounced as immoral. I am aware, of course, that few good men would have maintained these theories without modification; but brevity requires that they should be stated in a direct, even if a repulsive form. On the other hand, the fact that sacrifice and suffering for the sake of others is the law of human life, and that by the death of Christ the destructive power of sin has been done away with for all who are attached to Him by faith, gains fresh evidence for all thoughtful men. The lapse of time and its healing effects encourage the hope of a better presentment of the doctrine.

A second factor tending to the same result is a certain change which has come about in our view of sin. Mr. Gladstone, some years ago, noticed this change and deplored it. But, though it would be indeed deplorable if it implied a laxity in regard to sin itself, it may be only a truthful chastening of an exaggeration: it may mean, and we may trust generally does mean—(1) That the sense of God's Fatherhood, which these forty years have brought into prominence, makes us lay stress on that aspect of sin which treats it as the "ignorance" of "those who are out of the way," the object of His compassion and not only of His wrath; (2) that we learn to think of the fall of man as a stage in the progress from innocent unconsciousness of good and evil, through the law which gives a "knowledge of sin" ("when the commandment came, sin revived and I died"), but which is also a schoolmaster leading us to the higher state of faith; and (3) that we realise that the taking away of sin and condemnation is not the sole or chief object of the redemptive process, but that its final aim is that given in the words, "to purge the conscience, that we may serve the living God."

A third factor of modern thought is the doctrine of the immanence of God, which Archdeacon Wilson has lately made the basis of his Hulsean lectures on the Atonement; for this leads us to think not of a "transaction" by which a distant Being is induced to pardon us, but of the Father through the Son and the Spirit uniting Himself with us and doing away with our selfishness and all its results by the overpowering influence of self-sacrificing love.

A fourth tendency is that which makes the Incarnation rather than the Atonement the central fact of theology, and which, with Bishop Westcott, prolongs the idea of Incarnation, so as to make it the hallowing and uplifting power in humanity. This tendency is seen alike in men like Baur in Germany, and in more recent writers, both Roman Catholic and Anglican (see especially Oxenham's "Catholic Doctrine of the Atonement"). It is not God who needed to be propitiated, but man, and this was effected by the whole manifestation of Christ: "God was in Christ, reconciling the world to Himself." "The death of Christ," says Klee, as quoted by Baur (*Versöhnungslehre*, 747), "is not the cause which moves God, but the mediating cause in redemption. God is not favourable to us because Christ is ours, but Christ is ours because God is favourable to us."

We may refer in this connection to the presentation of the Atonement in the great work of Ritschl *(Rechtfertigung und Versöhnung)*, which may be summed up thus: That the object of the manifestation of Christ is the establishment of the Kingdom of God; that each soul has its proper place in the Kingdom; and that the Atonement is the restoration of each one to its proper place, involving justification and pardon, and also an impulse towards the goodness which is the essence of the kingdom.

We may recognise in all these tendencies, whatever weight we may assign to them, a demand for reality. "Let us have done with legal fictions," men seem to be saying, "and let us see the Atonement as a moral process which commends itself to our consciences."

No one can doubt the need of an Atonement if we take the word according to its derivation, which is another form of the older "onement," and means simply reconciliation, or bringing into harmony or union (see Murray's Dictionary). A moral reconciliation of heart and will is that which every man needs; and it includes the whole process by which faith is first engendered in the soul, and afterwards a man's will and affections and his whole life are "subdued to the obedience of Christ." In what sense we may speak of God also as reconciled to us, we will discuss later on. We cannot put this question aside, for the fears which have beset men's minds, and have only been pacified by the doctrine of the Atonement, have related primarily, not to their disposition towards God, but to God's disposition towards them. Nevertheless, it is a sound principle to begin with what is known and verifiable, and thence to gain an estimate of what is darker. Christ Himself taught us, in this very matter, to speak first of earthly things, and then of their heavenly counterpart (John iii. 11, 12, 14, 15).

Now, while the effect of the work of Christ on the mind of God has been felt to be so hard to understand that Bishop Butler thought it presumptuous to attempt to define it, the effect on the mind of each believer is a matter of distinct and daily experience. We come to Him who assures us that God is His Father and ours; we recognise His teaching as having on it the stamp of divinity; we see in His life and person the image of righteousness sublimated into love, of love passing into self-sacrifice; and His death is both the culmination of this and its conclusive test. By the whole process, but most of all by His death, we are humbled, awed, attracted, and filled with a longing to be like Him. "I, if I be lifted up from the earth, will draw all men unto Me." This is the process of Atonement or reconciliation from its earthly side, the side of human experience. It is fully recognised in the New Testament. Indeed, there are but few passages, even in the Epistles of St. Paul, relating to the Atonement in which this effect on the heart and life of men is not clearly brought out. "He died for all, that they who live should not henceforth live unto themselves, but unto Him which died for them and rose again."

Can we, then, say that this is all which

Atonement is henceforth to mean to us, and that we are no longer to speak of God as becoming propitious and forgiving through the sacrifice of Christ? I do not think such ideas or expressions will ever become unreal.

The self-condemning conscience, the haunting sense of guilt, cannot be pacified by any merely subjective process. It asks again and again, Can God really forgive me? and, if this question be not answered, men are thrown back continually upon some non-rational or non-moral explanation. It may, seem, indeed, presumptuous, as Bishop Butler said, to attempt to estimate the effect on the Divine mind of Christ's self-sacrifice; even Professor Jowett, in his celebrated Essay (lately reprinted in the new edition of his work on the Epistles of St. Paul), said that on this point we must "fall back on mystery"; and Dean Farrar is content to rest where Butler rested. But, as McLeod Campbell pointed out, the Scriptural writers do not hint at a mystery, but write as if every reader would understand them when they speak of Christ being "a propitiation set forth by God that He might justify all who believe in Him"; or of Christ's offering Himself to God, and "putting away sin by the sacrifice of Himself"; or of God "remembering no more our sins and iniquities."

Nor need we, in estimating this side of the Atonement, depart from the plain ground of moral convictions. It is true that God is without variableness or shadow of turning; He is unchangeable righteousness and love. But the same righteousness and love which beams upon the repentant and believing soul with forgiveness and complacency cannot but wear towards the rebellious, unloving spirit the aspect of displeasure. Repentance and faith change for us the face of God. And thus we may understand the passages which speak of this change. "God saw their works, that they turned from their evil ways, and God repented of the evil that He had said that He would do unto them, and He did it not."

If, then, the death of Christ, viewed as the culminating point of His life of love, is the destined means of repentance for the whole world, we may say, also, that it is the means of securing the mercy and favour of God, of procuring the forgiveness of sins. And then the sacrificial language of the apostolical epistles becomes full of meaning to us. Take such an expression as that of Hebrews ix. 23: "It was necessary that the heavenly things themselves should be cleansed with better sacrifices than these." The heavens and all that is in them, the aspect of God Himself, are lurid and dark till they are purged for us by that sacrifice which ensures alike our repentance and the favour of God. The sacrifice is not less real because it is the sacrifice of self. When, by the light of the Epistle to the Hebrews, we put aside the shadowy and unreal notions which beset the idea of sacrifice, and see that the true sacrifice is that of the man himself—"Lo, I come to do Thy will, O God"—we can understand that this return of filial obedience to the Father, as it has power over us, has power also with God. "The satisfaction," says McLeod Campbell, "was required not by a rigid law, but by a Father's heart."

A difficulty, however, occurs to us in this, that, whereas we have pointed first to the efficacy of the death of Christ on human beings, yet in the common conception, and at times in Scripture, its efficacy on the Divine nature is spoken of first, if not alone. But this difficulty, I think, can be explained. The sacrifice of Christ comes before its effects on us; and its effects on us are wrapped up in it, so that we may say without unreality that in the self-offering of Christ it is the human race itself which is returning to God. Christ stands for mankind, and we have a right to believe that God, because of Christ's self-sacrifice, forgives us all. We have a right to preach this, and the sinner who is beginning to return to God has a right to believe that through Christ's righteousness, not his own, he is saved. It is true that faith is always a moral act, and involves a complete adherence of the moral man to its object. But the weak believer cannot realise this. He can but say, "Help Thou mine unbelief"; and it is an inexpressible comfort to him to be able to stake everything, not on any moral result in himself, but upon the fact that Jesus has lived and died for him. Thus we may realise the value of the old Gospel message and retain the expressions which have been dear to so many generations.

It is possible, indeed, that future generations may not need these explanations, and that the sense of God's Fatherhood and His indwelling or immanence may become so habitual to those who have been brought up under the influence of a truer and simpler Christianity, that mercy and forgiveness will be presupposed from the first, and the whole stress of the Christian life be laid on the following of Christ. But we can hardly assume this. Through all these nineteen centuries the first great need of burdened souls has been to know that God has pardoned them, and to be assured of this, not by word, but by the sacrifice of the Cross. It is a great thing to Christian teachers to know that they can preach the Cross without any misrepresentation of the justice and the love of God.

But there is one point more of the utmost importance, to which the difficulty just stated points us. The effect of the Atonement is not primarily to save men from punishment and misery and to bring them into happiness, but to save them from alienation and to bring them into moral union with the righteousness and the love of God. (This has lately been insisted on very powerfully by Professor Sabatier, of Paris.) Those who have been driven away from the Christian profession by the crudeness with which the doctrine of the Atonement has been preached, are apt to speak of the statements of the apostles as if they implied that the object was to free men from eternal torments. I remember going through a number of texts which were put together as showing this, and it was evident that in almost every case there was no reference to the liberation from punishment, but from sin. For instance, the words of St. Peter (1 Peter i. 19), " Redeemed with the precious blood of Christ," were quoted without seeing that the redemption spoken of was "from your vain conversation received by tradition from your fathers"; or those of

Gal. i. 4, "Who gave Himself for our sins," without noticing the words "that He might deliver us from this present evil world." And it must be admitted that men are apt to cling merely to the negative side of the redemptive process and to stop at the forgiveness of sins, whereas the teaching of the apostles always points to, and almost always affirms, the positive side, and speaks of the Cross as the stimulus to righteousness and love and devoted service. Perhaps the most pregnant text in the Bible is Heb. ix. 14, "The blood of Christ, who through the eternal Spirit offered Himself without spot to God, shall purge your consciences from dead works to serve the living God." The offering is that of self, a moral act in contrast to the sacrifice of non-moral victims; its value lies in its being pure and immaculate; its results are, negatively, to purge the conscience and, positively, to lead us into the service of God.

And this redemptive process is not merely individual; it extends to the race of mankind and to the whole constitution of things in which we live. "God sent His Son . . . that *the world* through Him might be saved"; "By Him to reconcile all things to Himself, whether they be things in earth or things in heaven." The Atonement is the stimulus to every effort for social regeneration, for freedom, for international peace, for the bending of all the forces of Nature to their proper object—the bringing in of the Kingdom of Christ. Let me refer to Mr. Peyton's remarkable articles in *The Contemporary Review* for April and May on "The Crucifixion as an Evolutionary Force." The more this positive and far-reaching aspect of the Atonement is dwelt upon the less likely we shall be to fall back into the puerile or immoral explanations which have obscured it, and the more powerful will it become for the work of Christian expansion and Christian unity, which is the task of this generation.

IX.

BY MARCUS DODS, D.D.,

Professor of New Testament Exegesis in New College, Edinburgh.

It is remarkable that the death of Christ, on which all Christians depend for salvation, and which might therefore be expected to be the most intelligible of all events, is actually one of the most obscure. But it is obscure partly because of its universal significance. There are so many different aspects in which it may be viewed, and so many various directions in which its influence applies itself, that it is impossible to give any definition of its significance comprehensive enough to include all, impossible to do more than recognise its significance from one point of view. This is all that can be attempted in this paper.

In speaking of the death of Christ it will be understood that this term is not intended to signify only that which happened on the cross, but rather all the obedience and suffering which led up to and were consummated and signalised in the actual crucifixion. The

all apprehend that it is a manifestation of God's love, but not that merely. Jesus claimed to be the Messiah, the Christ, the chosen and anointed representative of God. It was this which gave significance and supreme importance to His death as to all He did and said. He died as Messiah or Christ. In His death it is not merely the love of a human heart, of man to man, He is expressing; it is the love of the unseen Father manifesting itself to His children. Take away the Messiahship, put aside the representative character of all that Jesus said and did, think of Him as a mere man and not as the revealer of God, and you destroy the radical and essential significance of His death. This act has universal significance, a message to all men, because it is the act of Him with whom all men have to do. It speaks to us of Divine sympathy, of Divine love and efficiency. It is the supreme expression of the Divine nature and of the Divine attitude towards us. Here we find God, and find Him in such an attitude towards us that we are overwhelmed with contrition, and at the same time have all hope and life renewed in us by the recognition of His sufficiency.

But while the death of Christ carries with it this grand result of revealing God's fatherly compassion and sacrifice, this cannot be said to be its primary object. It does convince us that God is Love and to be depended upon to the uttermost; but had it been contrived solely for the purpose of producing this persuasion, manifestly it would not have done so. I understand and appreciate the devotion and affection of the man who steps in between my breast and a bayonet-thrust; but I am only bewildered if he seeks to prove his love for me by exposing himself needlessly when I am in no danger. I need no explanation of the self-sacrifice of the man who springs into the water to rescue me from certain death, but if while I am safe on land, and in order to prove his love for me, he leaps into a torrent no swimmer can stem and is lost, I fail to perceive his sanity and can only lament his useless act. We cannot lower the death of Christ to the level of such superfluous and irrelevant displays, but must believe that there was a need for the sacrifice, and that the love in it was manifested by the recognition and satisfaction of the need.

The questions remains, then, what was the need and how did Christ's death satisfy it? There was need of some such demonstration of God's righteousness as would make it possible and safe for Him to forgive the unrighteous. In order that God's love might find free expression in the forgiveness of His children two things at least were necessary—that they should be penitent, and that they should be actually and powerfully impelled towards righteousness. Bare forgiveness, the mere proclamation of free pardon to all, could accomplish neither of these ends. It could not secure adequate repentance, and it could not secure righteousness. The death of Christ secures both. Let us see how.

First, Repentance. In order to forgiveness there must be repentance, the keen sense that sin is against God and separates from Him, and the earnest craving for reconcilement.

Without this there can be no forgiveness. A man cannot be admitted into the favour of God without the earnest desire for it. Forgiveness means nothing, and cannot come into operation where impenitence continues.

But if it is inconceivable that God should forgive the impenitent, it is equally inconceivable that He should not forgive the penitent. "The Lord is nigh unto them that are of a broken heart and saveth such as be of a contrite spirit." It cannot be otherwise. The object of all God's dealings is to win us to Himself and to separate us from sin. And when the sinner desires above all else to be reconciled to God his return is eagerly welcomed. However seriously a person has injured you, and however just and keen your resentment is, you cannot cherish anger when you see him truly penitent, crushed with shame, doing all that lies in his power to compensate for the wrong done.

> Who is not with repentance satisfied
> Is not of heaven nor earth.

To cherish resentment against the penitent, is

to cherish resentment against the dead, for the disposition which prompted the injury is now non-existent. It is another, a new man that is now before you, a man who hates what the old man did, and would spend himself in repairing the wrong done. To cherish resentment and withold forgiveness in such a case is fatuous and devilish. True penitence is, in short, irresistible. It is the real solvent of past discord.

But apart from the Cross of Christ, or from those foreshadowings of it in the Old Testament which produced the same or a similar impression of God's righteousness, there is no adequate repentance. Repentance can never be adequate until the perception of God's righteousness is adequate. The Cross, exhibiting at once the righteousness and the love of God, is the supreme and perfect instrument for producing repentance. It can never be surpassed, but stands to all time as the sufficient means for bringing to men the knowledge and hatred of their own evil. Here men learn that God grudges no sacrifice by which righteousness can be promoted; that it is, therefore, His supreme interest. Here His righteousness and His love are seen to be inextricably intertwined, both alike prompting Him above all else to seek by righteous methods for the righteousness of men. In point of fact, it is only in Christendom worthy repentance has been found, and it is at the Cross that Christians have found it. By being the source, then, of true and fruitful penitence, the death of Christ removes the radical subjective obstacle in the way of forgiveness.

Second, the death of Christ not only makes forgiveness possible by producing the penitence which alone can crave and accept it, but also it secures that forgiveness shall not be abused. It safeguards morality, law, righteousness. The question is not whether God desired to forgive, but whether it was possible for Him to forgive without at the same time introducing to men's minds a deeper reverence for righteousness. Constituted as men are, mere impunity would have led to further transgression, to disbelief in the reality of law and righteousness. Forgiveness, in order to be safe from abuse, must reach men in such a way as shall more deeply impress them with the value of righteousness than their own punishment would have done. Proclamation of universal pardon without any accompanying exhibition of the sacredness of law must have resulted in a lowering of all sense of right. It is not that God is implacable and must be propitiated, but that the moral well-being of man requires that it be clearly exhibited that the demand of perfect righteousness is not too severe, and that human blessedness consists not in escaping but in acknowledging and possessing righteousness. We can be forgiven at the foot of the Cross, because in the Cross we see the result of sin and the sacredness of law. We there see what sin actually does, involving in its misery the highest and best of beings. We can be pardoned because the Cross humbles us, convinces us that righteousness is supreme, and binds us by every good bond to Him who makes His Spirit ours.

Or to put it in a slightly different form, God cannot pass by our transgressions and treat us as if we were His dear and loyal children, without at the same time showing us that He does not make light of transgression nor set aside the law of righteousness on which our purity and happiness depend. Forgiveness must come through a medium which safeguards righteousness. The substitution of Christ's death for our punishment answers this purpose. It more effectually binds us to God and righteousness than our own punishment would have done. It is not our physical suffering God desires; it is our permanent establishment in that holiness that unites to Himself and makes us sharers in His blessedness. This He accomplishes by Christ's interposition.

The two great ends of punishment, the homage to law and the reformation of the law-breaker, are thus alike secured by the death of Christ. The radical idea and essential element in punishment is the establishment of law, the impression conveyed that law is law and cannot with impunity be broken. It is on the stability of law or right that human happiness depends. Dismiss the sanctity of law and you cut human hope down at the root. But punishment may also reform the criminal. Rarely does it accomplish this end indeed, but it may legitimately be hoped for and aimed at. The death of Christ secures both ends in the highest degree.

The death of Christ, then, has made forgiveness possible, because it enables men to repent with an adequate penitence, and because it magnifies righteousness and binds men to God. We have now to ask what it was in the death of Christ which accomplishes these ends. What relation precisely had Christ's suffering to our own? What is the element in Christ's suffering which differentiates it from that of other men and gives it saving significance? This may be answered in a word—it was its voluntariness, or, which is the same thing, its representative character.

We have recognised that as Messiah or Christ Jesus lived and acted as God's representative, but as Christ He was also man's representative. He was so not by any formal investiture, but by being what all men ought to be and by becoming the source of a new creation, a new life and type of man. He claims that His death was a death for the race, His blood is shed for many. This implies a relation to the race not sustained by ordinary men. It implies that in some sense He represents the race. Coming to the world as the Christ, He undertakes to satisfy on man's behalf the whole will of God. And it is in this capacity He dies. It is this which explains His anxiety and agony. To compare His death with that of Socrates is absurd. Socrates died for himself alone; his own reputation, but little else, depended on his firmness in dying. Jesus knew Himself to be the Christ, the representative of all men, and knew, therefore, that on His constancy and submission in dying depended the hope of mankind. It was this responsibility, together with the sense that death was the fruit of sin and embodied "the curse," that crushed Him with a burden He could scarcely sustain.

By submitting to all God's appointments without a murmur, by allowing the consequences of sin to find expression in His own life and death, He owned God's righteousness and magnified the law. By assuming our place, by showing us that our sin strikes God Himself and involves in its consequences Him who best loves us, He humbles us as nothing else can humble us, and brings us to sincere repentance. It is the voluntariness of His suffering that touches, softens and purifies.

It may further be asked, In what sense can we say that Christ suffered our punishment? We can certainly say it in the sense that all Christ's suffering was the consequence of human sin. His suffering was the inevitable result of His presence in an evil world. Human sin is punished not by any direct interposition and infliction at God's hand, but by the natural consequences that result. These consequences fell on Christ, so that while we cannot say that He was punished, because this would imply that He had sinned, we can say that He suffered the punishment of human sin.

There are passages in the epistles of St. Paul

which, when read by themselves, seem to give us the baldest and bluntest doctrine of substitution. He goes so far as to say that Christ was made sin for us, that He became a curse for us. Separated from the spiritual condition and experience of him who used these expressions they appear repellent. Even so profound and serious a theologian as Dr. Martineau exclaims: "How is the alleged immorality of letting off the sinner mended by the added crime of penalty crushing the sinless? Of what man—of what angel—could such a thing be reported without raising a cry of indignant shame from the universal human heart? What should we think of a judge who should discharge the felons from the prisons of a city because some noble and generous citizen offered himself to the executioner instead?" But we cannot by so easy a use of analogies dispose of Paul's statements. In any case we have this fact to explain—that a perfectly sinless person suffered and died an ignominious death. Here also, at first sight, we seem to be confronted with a flagrant injustice. What is its explanation? Paul says He suffered in our room.

This, like every other part of Paul's teaching, is explained by the central fact of his Christian experience, his union with Christ. The motto of his Christian life was, "I in Christ, Christ in me"; there was no fact of which he was more certain than that he and Christ were one, inextricably united. How he arrived at this conviction cannot here be detailed. But that from it many consequences resulted is apparent. And one of these consequences was that he felt it to be the most natural thing in the world that what Christ did and suffered should be valid for him. He could not think of Christ as one person, and himself as another. His personality was embraced in Christ's. With such presuppositions substitution becomes quite another thing. Besides, when Dr. Martineau compares Christ's substitution to the substitution of a noble citizen in the room of gaolfuls of felons, he excites a prejudice against the Atonement by a false analogy. The noble citizen has no means of securing that the felons acquitted should also be transformed into virtuous citizens; but the very nerve of Christ's substitution lies in this, that He was able, and in thousands of instances has made good His ability, to make new men of those for whom He died. Society is no doubt injured if one citizen capable of heroism, which his country may urgently need at some crisis of its fortunes, be sacrificed to give to a troop of worthless men a liberty which they will abuse for every evil purpose. But this bears no analogy to a substitution of which the main intended and actual result is to make good men; a substitution which takes effect and frees from punishment only those who are thus renewed, and which indeed is the only agency ever discovered which does renew large numbers of men. Christ's substitution is justified by the fact that He was able to secure that greater moral results would from it accrue to the race than could be reached by punishment of the sinner.

X.

BY AUGUSTE SABATIER,

Dean of the Faculty of Protestant Theology of the University of Paris.

IN the first contribution which appeared in *The Christian World* on this great subject Mr. Campbell very properly drew attention to the prevalence of the doctrine of Expiation in the tradition of the Christian Church. But it has not always been the same doctrine, at least, so far as its expression is concerned. The doctors of the Middle Ages formulated and justified it in a fashion different from that followed by the Church Fathers, while we in our turn conceive it quite otherwise than did the Middle Ages. To exhibit this evolution will not be to contradict Mr. Campbell's exposition, but to complete it. It will not, moreover, affect the doctrine of any particular Church, because while all the Churches have established a certain necessary connection between the death of Christ and the pardon of sin, none of them has introduced into its *credo*, or sanctioned as an article of faith, any precise formula of expiation. One theory after another has in turn been allowed to prevail, and modern orthodoxy has on this subject become distinctly broad and tolerant. We may therefore discuss with entire liberty the successive ways in which theologians have expounded the doctrine.

Their explanations arrange themselves under two leading types, which are the expression of two radically opposed views. According to the one the death of Christ has procured the pardon of sins, because it has influenced the mind of God and induced Him to forgive. Divine grace has here its primary cause in the expiation furnished by Jesus Christ. According to the other view, Divine grace, the mercy of God from whence pardon proceeds, is absolute, depending on nothing else than itself; it remains the all-sufficient cause, the *primum movens* of the redemption of sinners. The death of Jesus is the outcome of grace, the historical means by which redemption is rendered effective. In other words, either we say that God forgives sinners because the death of Christ has paid their debt to His justice; or we reverse the relation, and say that Jesus died as the result of God's will to pardon. These two points of view imply in reality two very different conceptions of Christianity itself, the juridic and legalist conception which predominated in the Early Church, and the ethical conception which tends to prevail in modern times. It is in the slow and painful movement from the first of these views to the other that the evolution of Christian thought upon this subject may be said to consist.

I. As a result of the Eucharist being understood and celebrated from an early period as an expiatory sacrifice, the view of the faithful in the Church of the first ages was directed to the Cross as the centre both of worship and of faith. But the need of seeking its precise significance and end was hardly felt. Gregory Nazianzen *(Orat.* 33) regards the subject as "a theme for free speculation." Accordingly, we find in the writings of the Fathers an extraordinary variety and fluctuation of opinion. It is to be observed that the so-called Apostle's Creed does not establish any relation between the death of Christ and the remission of sins; and that the Nicene-Constantinopolitan Creed rests the work of redemption at once on the incarnation, the sufferings, the death, and the resurrection of the Son of God. The dominant conception, nevertheless, is that of a ransom paid to Satan, and it is curious to observe how, in this theory, the forensic idea is mixed up with a mythological representation of the Divine relationship to the devil.

Satan has taken possession of humanity, which he holds captive. He has over it a right of legitimate possession. And God does not use violence to eject him from his claim. The Just One will, in His dealing with the unjust, use the forms of justice. He proposes therefore to the adversary a bargain; He offers to him the soul of the Son of God as a ransom for human souls, and it is on this account that the Son dies and descends into Hades. It is not God's fault if Satan has not the power

to detain the Redeemer in prison—if the
latter breaks the gates of hell and destroys the
power of its king. Satan has made a fool's
bargain, but for that he has only himself to
blame. He has rightfully lost everything as
the price of his measureless ambition
(Irenæus Ad Haer, V. I. I. Origen in Matt. xii. 8.
Gregory of Nyssa Or. Catech. 22-26*)*.

This theory of Divine manœuvre did not,
however, universally satisfy. Augustine is
scandalised with it. But he, while affirming
that Christ had paid the ransom of sinners to
the Divine justice, and not to the devil, did not
see very clearly the necessity for this ransom.
He declares in one place that God was free to
choose, in His grace, other means of redemption, and that if He has chosen the death of
Christ, it is because He so willed, and that He
desired to win us by His love (*August, De
Agone Christi II., De Catechiz* 7).

It is with Anselm of Canterbury, at the end
of the eleventh century, in the famous treatise,
Cur Deus Homo, that the doctrine of Expiation
takes precise and definite form as a theory of

equivalent satisfaction given by the Son of God to Divine justice. This theory has for basis and point of departure the Germanic penal law. Every offence demands a reparation, and this reparation may be furnished either by the punishment of the culprit or by a compensation offered to the injured party equivalent to the injury he has suffered. Man has, by his sin, offended the honour of God. This honour being infinite, the offence committed becomes of infinite gravity, and can be repaired only by infinite and eternal pains endured by the offender, unless he can furnish to God an exact reparation. Man would never be able to do this because, were he henceforth perfectly obedient, he owes this obedience naturally to God, and consequently cannot in this way obtain any excess of merit whereby to pay off the antecedent debt. Man is, then, irremediably lost unless God Himself come to his aid. Only a God could acquire an infinite merit, but it would be necessary also that this God should at the same time be man, because it is a human debt that is to be paid. Thus, then, was it an absolute necessity that the Son of God should become incarnate. It is further to be noted here that it is not by His virtues, by His active obedience, that Christ acquires His merits before God, for He owes this obedience to God on His own account. It is by His sufferings and by His death. Being without sin, He was under no obligation either to suffer or to die. If, then, He accepts suffering and death, He obtains thereby an excess of merit available for the service of sinners. This merit is infinite, for the sufferings and death of a God have an infinite value. They more than cover the debt of man. That debt to the Divine justice is accordingly now entirely liquidated; the reparation has been made by a satisfactory equivalent. Man may now be saved. Herein is revealed the double necessity for the incarnation and for the death of the Son of God.

That this theory, with the slight modification brought to it by Thomas Aquinas, should have become the orthodox one of the Roman Catholic Church is in no way surprising. Romanism found here the best possible support for its doctrine of the efficacy of the Mass and for the practice of indulgences. Nor need we wonder that this fashion of considering sin as a debt to be paid, and the application of Divine grace as a credit transfer, should have satisfied the superstitious piety and the inferior morality of the Middle Ages. Anselm's theory, indeed, marked a real progress over that of the Church Fathers. What does astonish us is that the Reformers, Luther especially, should have received it with such eagerness, and that the Protestant theologians of the seventeenth century should have defended it, in an even exaggerated form, with such tenacity. They were seduced, no doubt, by the awful emphasis which the theory placed upon sin, and the impossibility of self-salvation to which it reduced the sinner. But the idea of sin which it offered, serious though it was, stood quite outside man himself. Sin offends the Divine honour, but there is no mention of its wounding, corrupting effect upon human nature. Accordingly it leaves no logical ground for repentance and reconciliation. The penalty alone enters into consideration. This having been once for all endured by the Son of God, and the debt paid, man may claim entrance into heaven, not as a grace, but as a right, in the name of the same justice that first of all condemned him, St. Paul would say, "We are here under the law, not under grace."

Anselm's theory is, in fact, irretrievably compromised in the presence of modern religious thought, and that it is so is owing not so much to the criticisms, weighty though they were, urged by the Socinians, Arminians and Rationalists of the eighteenth century as to the fact that it is absolutely contrary to the fundamental postulates of Scripture, as well as to those of the Christian conscience. It is the idea of grace itself that is here attacked. The more strict and logical the form in which the penal law theory of equivalent satisfaction is presented, the more completely is grace excluded from it. Where a satisfaction has been offered there can be no question of grace. When the creditor has been paid, he is showing no grace to the debtor in holding him free of obligation. A God who pardons because He has been satisfied, and after he has been satisfied, does not really pardon at all. In fact, in this theory the idea of grace and of free pardon can only be preserved by saying that God has paid to Himself the satisfaction which He demanded of man. This, however, from the legal point of view on which the theory is constructed, is nonsense, a trifling emptied of all reality. When it has reached this point the theory has contradicted and destroyed itself.

Both the word and the idea of satisfaction, thus understood, are foreign to the Bible. In the Scriptures man's salvation and the pardon of his sin always proceed from an initial act of pure mercy. Their primary cause is a gracious decision of the Divine love, beyond which it is impossible to go. God pardons because He loves and He loves because He is Love. It is from his paternal heart that the work of redemption has sprung. In the Old Testament everything proceeds from this free, sovereign, and absolute grace—the Covenant with Israel, the promises made to the fathers and to the children, the deliverances granted, the sins forgotten or remitted. For the manifestation of this infinite mercy no other condition is required than the repentance of the people, their return to God, their confidence in the grace of God. When we inquire closely we discover that the expiatory sacrifices themselves have no efficiency except in virtue of this Divine mercy, and that they serve not so much for satisfying God as for manifesting the repentance and faith of man. And this explains why they remain without virtue, and, indeed, become obnoxious to God when they are offered by worshippers who have not repented and whose hearts are hardened *(Exod.* xix. 4-6, xxxiv. 5, 10; *Deut.* v. 2, *et seq.; Hosea* v. 6, vi. 6; *Micah* vi. 6-16; *Amos* v. 21; *Isaiah* l. 10-26; *Jeremiah* vi. 20; *Ps.* xl. 6, 7, xlix. 7, 8, li. 16-19, *&c., &c.).*

And if the free initiative of God's grace is seen in the beginning of the Old Covenant, much more is it visible throughout the whole course of the New. It would be superfluous to insist upon, or to prove that Jesus in His preaching makes the forgiveness of sins, the publication of the good news of the kingdom, and the salvation of sinners to rest upon the free and gracious decision of His Father. Nothing is further from His thought than to lay down as a necessary condition of that grace a previously demanded satisfaction on the part of God. The Father pardons; He opens His arms to the prodigal simply because He is God, and that He wills not the death of a sinner, but His conversion and his life *(Matt.* xi. 25, *et seq.; Luke* vii. 41-50; xv. 12-32). When Jesus declares, in another place, that He " gives His life a ransom for many," the very form of this partial declaration ($\dot{a}\nu\tau\grave{\iota}\ \pi o\lambda\lambda\hat{\omega}\nu$) and the context proves that what He here speaks of is His love, which devotes itself to His brethren, and that the ransom He pays is to His brethren, and not to God. So in His words at the Last Supper, if the New Covenant is to be sealed with His blood, this Covenant is essentially a gift of Divine grace, a gift not evoked by the death of Christ, but that is by that death introduced and realised in human history. It is enough to note here the "royal text" in this matter: "God so loved the world that He gave His Son" (*John* iii. 16). The death of Jesus is not the cause which moves the love of God; it is the love of God which is the cause of Christ's coming and of His death.

What, too, of the idea of grace as presented in the teaching of St. Paul? The Epistles to the Romans, to the Galatians, and to the Ephesians might be cited entire to show that the χάρις τοῦ θεοῦ brought by Christ to sinners, whether considered as individuals, as nations, or as humanity together, proceeds solely from the Divine εὐδοκία (*Eph.* i. 5, 6, *Phil.* i. 28, *comp. John* v. 36, xi. 42; 1 *John* iv. 9). There is, then, in the whole Christian revelation nothing more solidly based than this. Everything in the Divine Dispensations for the salvation of men is derived from the Divine grace, while that is itself underived. It is not the death of Christ which determines grace; it is grace that determines and brings to pass the death of Christ.

It may be objected that there are other and
very numerous declarations in the New Testament where the death of Jesus is assimilated
to the expiatory sacrifices of the Old Testament; where the blood of Christ is represented as covering and effacing sin. Has not
Christ been made sin and a curse for us ? Has
He not borne our sins in His body on the tree ?
(*Gal.* iii. 13; 2 *Cor.* v. 21; *Col.* ii. 14; 1 *John*
i. 7; *Heb.* ix. 12-16; 1 *Peter* i. 2, 19, &c.;
Rev. i. 5). But this second series of passages
is not necessarily contradictory of the first.
A harmony can without difficulty be established between them, provided we are determined not to interpret the Christian revelation
according to certain Levitical texts, but rather
to study these, and all the comparisons or
images drawn from them by the Apostles in
the spirit of the Christian revelation. For instance, to touch only the essential point, it is
evident that in the parallel drawn between the
ancient sacrifices and that of Calvary, there is
to be found always one vital distinction. In
the old sacrifices the victim is devoted to death

contrary to its will ; it is recalcitrant under the knife of the sacrificer. In the sacrifice of Calvary the Victim is not devoted; He devotes Himself. His death is a manifestation of love; and if it is asked in what consists the superiority of Christ's sacrifice the answer is precisely in this act of love in the gift of Himself. This love constitutes the very essence, the whole expiatory virtue, of His death. Take away in thought the love from that death and we have in this bleeding, agonising punishment no more expiatory virtue than in the blood of bulls or of goats. It follows from this that the physical suffering, the bloodshed, have no other *rôle* than that of symbols, or rather of vivid expressions; pathetic manifestations, of the love of Christ. The greater the suffering of Christ the more are we moved by it because it shows to us how much he has loved us.

But the death of Christ, while, according to Scripture, a manifestation of ineffable love, is, at the same time, not less a condemnation of sin. The sinner sees here his soul loved by another, who gives Himself entirely for his salvation; he finds also his sin made manifest in all its murderous strength and utter culpability. He is then in a double sense associated with the suffering of Him who is at once the Holy and the Loving One. Yet the condemnation does not consist in the amount of the suffering endured by the Redeemer, but in the sense of the guilt of sin awakened in the heart of the sinner. The triumph of Divine justice through love consists in this, that the sin condemned objectively by the Cross is condemned also subjectively in the conscience of the Christian, who by a profound inner return to God breaks with his own sin, dies to sin, to rise unto newness of life (*Romans* vi. 1-7). We need to enter into the Pauline idea of the mystical union of Christ with sinners by love, and of the mystical union of sinners with Christ crucified by repentance and faith, to get the true notion according to Paul of the justice of God, a justice which is not solely a power of punishment, but a *justice that justifies*, that is, which triumphs over evil in the hearts even of evil doers. (εἰς τὸ εἶναι Θεὸν δίκαιον καὶ δικαιοῦντα τὸν ἐκ πίστεως.—Romans iii. 26.) The Pauline δικαιοσύνη Θεοῦ mediates between the ὀργὴ Θεοῦ, which is the negative reaction of God against sin, and the χάρις τοῦ Θεοῦ, His love of the sinner. The δικαιοσύνη Θεοῦ saves the sinner, not by obtaining as satisfaction the quantity of suffering merited by his sin, but by destroying at once the guilt of sin and the sin itself. And this is the true expiation. For sin is only really expiated by reparation, that is to say, by being abolished.

To sum up here the principal points in the Scriptural doctrine in contrast with that of Anselm:

1. The idea of a necessarily and preliminary satisfaction, in Anselm's sense, is foreign to the Bible, and contrary to the Christian notion of the absolute sovereign liberty of the grace of God.

2. In the Bible God is not presented as a pitiless judge who punishes and curses a criminal in the person of Christ crucified, but as a Father who accepts the devotion of the Son of His love.

3. The distinction between an *obedientia activa* on the part of Christ, due from Him to God, and an *obedientia passiva* which would secure for Him a surplus of merit with God available for sinners, is absolutely foreign to the Bible. The very words, "Christ's merits," in the mediæval sense are contrary to Scripture.

4. The idea of Christ's substitution for the sinner, and of the sinner's substitution for Christ before God, is in conformity with the Biblical view if we understand it not as a legal fiction arbitrarily imposed by a judge in a law court, but as a moral reality created on the one side by the love of Christ in its union with man, and on the other by the faith of the believer which associates itself with the sufferings and death of Christ, "dying and rising again with Him."

From all this it results that the theory of "satisfaction" no longer remains valid to Christian thought.

If now we are asked to define the direction in which modern theology has, on this subject, been moving for the last century—the general aim represented by its endeavours—the reply is not difficult. The capital defect of the old theory lay in its legal character. The Christian thought of our time has, on the contrary, been constantly endeavouring to lift the doctrine of expiation from the forensic to the ethical point of view. It has sought to substitute in the processes of the work of redemption the realities of the moral life for the abstract fictions created by logic in the name of human penal law. Whether it be in dealing with God Himself, or with the work of Christ, or with the justification of man, the Christian conscience remains unsatisfied so long as it has not discovered everywhere the living action of the moral laws, until it has transformed expiation from a metaphysical or juridical drama into that moral action which alone can have any positive efficacy. To understand expiation in this true sense is to bring heaven to earth, to weave the transcendental into the fibre of human history. This is not to attenuate the work of Christ. But it makes clear to us what is the object of that work, which is not to appease God and to reconcile Him with men, but to reconcile man with God. In the dying Christ God, according to the words of Paul, was already present in all His love, "working directly to reconcile sinners with Himself." (2 *Cor.* v. 19.)

One of the results following from the adoption of the ethical point of view is the disappearance of the abstract conflict which obtained in the old theory between God's justice and His love. The Divine justice would be inferior to that of man if it were purely negative and punitory, if it had not as its ultimate end the conquest of evil by good; in other words, if the penalty it inflicts on sin had not, in the final analysis, an educative intention looking towards moral elevation and salvation. On this side, then, the justice of God is already His love. But a Divine love which was no more than a simple indulgence, which suppressed pain while not removing sin, would be inferior to the genuine love of a human father, who knows perfectly well that sparing his child would be quite different from saving him, unless pardon had the effect of causing his repentance and amendment. So that on the other side the love of God is again His justice. It is accordingly a pure legal fiction to oppose one to the other, and to undertake the task, at once superfluous and impossible, of reconciling them. It was not the object of Christ's death to modify the Divine disposition, but to demonstrate on what conditions God's pardon might be realised in the conscience: by the condemnation, namely, of sin by the sinner himself, and consequently the actual destruction of the sin.

Another fiction possible from the penal point of view, but impossible from the ethical one, is that of conceiving the penalty as separable from the sin, or merit as an entity transferable from one to another. In the moral order the first and most serious of sin's penalties is, not external suffering or physical death, but the inner consciousness of guilt, that inward malediction which lives in the sinner's conscience. The moral lapse thus carries its punishment in itself. Hence not only would it be unjust to punish the innocent; but, what is more, it is actually impossible, for the simple reason that an innocent person cannot have the conscience of a guilty one. Christ might be condemned by a human tribunal: He could not be condemned by God. It was possible for Him to suffer injustice in the death of the Cross; but it was impossible for Him to bear suffering as a punishment.

On the same ground it would be also a fiction to regard a sin as really absolved by the remission of the external suffering attached to it, while the guilt and tyranny of the sin still remained. As long as a man feels himself guilty he does not realise pardon. Accordingly the emphasis of atonement lies, not so much in the quantity of pain suffered as in the abolition of the guilt itself. In order that there may be no more fiction in the Christian pardon than there is in the sense of guilt felt after sin it is not enough that Christ dies for us; it is also absolutely necessary that, as St. Paul says, we die with Him, that our faith and repentance make redemption actual in our conscience, effacing in us, as by a death, the consequences of sin, and creating in us, as by a kind of moral resurrection, a new life. The atonement is to be understood as taking place *in* us and not outside us. It is only on this condition that it acquires an ethical character and an ethical value.

The death of Jesus, then, is not the metaphysical cause which disposes God to pardon, but it is the essential historical condition without which the plan of grace could not have come to realisation. It is organically related to sin as the effect to its cause. But there is no need, in order to the understanding of this relation, to attach to it some transcendent drama in the Divine nature.

The conditions of the moral development of humanity sufficiently explain the necessity for the death of Jesus. To understand that word of His that "the Son of Man must suffer many things and be put to death," it is enough to remember what He was and what was the moral and social environment in which He lived. The wisdom of Plato had already seen and said that one perfectly just could not appear amongst the senseless and the wicked without provoking a murderous hatred. It is a general law of history that no one can hope to accomplish good amongst men without suffering with and for them. The special element in the life and work of Christ lies in the fact that He accepted voluntarily, and considered as His mission, the bearing of the whole weight of this burden of human solidarity. The hard and fatal fact of this organic solidarity was in Him transformed by Conscience into a moral duty. It was His personal love that consecrated in death the bond between His holy life and the destiny of sinners, a love which brought upon Himself all the misery that weighed on them. This love made of His entire life from beginning to end a sacrifice, and this sacrifice He himself voluntarily offered, not to God, who had no need of it, not to the devil, who had no right to it, but to His brethren whom He wished thus to deliver not merely from the penalty of sin, but from the sin itself. By His love He has entered into union with our sins that we by repentance and faith might have union with His righteousness.

To make expiation in this way a work of the love of Christ is not to annul it. It is, on the contrary, to deepen its tragedy while it heightens its efficacy. It is no longer a matter simply of the endurance of penalty, but of the deliverance of the sinner and the annihilation of his sin.

This transformation of the doctrine has for one of its results the re-establishment of the moral unity of Christ's life and work, a unity which the old theology, by its distinction between the passive and the active obedience, had broken. Passive obedience! Is not that a contradiction in terms? When was the soul of Jesus more active, when did it display more of moral energy and holy heroism than in the week of the Passion and during the hours of agony upon the Cross? It is only by a violent fiction that His death can be isolated from the rest of His life, as though this last had not been always the offering of Himself, as though He had not made of His death the supreme act of His life. That death has, no doubt, an exceptional place and value, but solely because it concentrates and expresses within itself, in a manner definitive and absolute, the sacrifice of His whole life.

In the next place, expiation, regarded in this way as an act essentially moral and human, relates itself to the universal law of the moral world, a law that rules us all and always, and which determines that those who love shall suffer in themselves a part, greater or less, of what is suffered by those whom they seek to save. The world becomes delivered from the burden of its sin and misery by the innocent and devoted love of those who charge themselves with it. The mother suffers for her erring son, and reclaims him by that suffering. That is the general law of redemption by love. However supernatural and unique the way in which we represent it, the expiatory work of Jesus is neither isolated nor incomprehensible. It is related to the law which it reveals and compels us to accept, that all love pays a ransom proportioned to its intensity and devotion. The sacrifice of Christ is the great redeeming sacrifice, because, while this love is only partial amongst the best of other men and full of reserves, His love was perfect and His gift of Himself absolute.

Jesus, then, remains the Chief in Redemption, the Conqueror of sin and death. But He is no longer alone. He associates in His work all His true disciples who have learned of Him to love and to devote themselves. To each of them He has given His cross to bear, and every cross, in the Christ-sense, is a means of redemption. The apostle Paul expresses this idea in a passage the virile energy of which gives almost a shock to our cold faith: " I rejoice in the sufferings which I endure for your sakes ($\dot{v}\pi\epsilon\rho$ $\dot{v}\mu\hat{\omega}\nu$), fulfilling thus in my flesh what is lacking in the sufferings of Christ, for His body's sake, which is the Church " (*Col.* i. 24). Hence it is not simply His teaching which Jesus charges His followers to perpetuate in the world ; it is also His never-completed suffering and death. It is not simply the prophet Christ who lives again in the immortal body of His Church; it is also, and above all (or at least ought to be), the sacrificial Christ who continues His suffering and death in His disciples, offering to the end, in them and for them, the holy Sacrament of His love until the redemption of humanity is fulfilled.

We have now stated what seem the authentic findings of the Christian conscience on this subject. If we are not disposed to stop here; if, going beyond the results of experience, we further inquire whence comes that supreme law of the moral world which imposes upon love this sacrifice of self as the price of redemption, we have only to recognise and confess our incompetence. On this question of the higher metaphysics, we find no reply that satisfies us. For my own part I stop, I confess, at the point beyond which the solid ground slips from under one's feet, and I reply with Jesus, "Even so, Father, because so has it seemed good in Thy sight." The question is, in effect, whether this law has not for end as much the development of the spiritual life as the punishment of sin. We come in contact here, indeed, with the mystery of the Divine creation itself. It would be rash in the extreme to draw conclusions as to the constitutive laws of the world from the experience that is specifically Christian. Human logic is too narrow and too superficial for this work. A sound critical theory of religious knowledge should lead us above all things, to soberness and to distrust of ourselves. Our anthropomorphic representations of God, of His action and of His designs, are inadequate and may very easily become contradictory. God's ways are not our ways, nor His thoughts our thoughts. Before these mysteries the intellect of the most learned as much as that of the humblest, stands baffled. To us all, whether we be great or little, there remains only the privilege of practical piety. It is ours to contemplate the work of Divine grace in history; to receive it into our hearts, and to recognise it as the object of our adoring gratitude.

XI.

BY WASHINGTON GLADDEN, D.D.

SPIRITUAL death is the wages of sin. It is not an arbitrary infliction, it is a natural consequence. Spiritual death manifests itself in the loss of spiritual insight, the increasing insensibility to all highest truth, the corruption of the desires, the perversion of the affections and a progressive state of moral degradation. The man who refuses to make love for God and his neighbour the supreme law of this life is suffering these consequences of his disobedience. The degrading effect of selfishness upon the evil-doer is immediate and inevitable; it can no more be denied by any sane man than the law of falling bodies can be denied.

A society composed of individuals who are in this condition will be full of confusion and every evil work. Selfish and jealous of one another, hateful and hating one another, corrupt and defiling one another, the members of such a society, by the terrible reactions of sin, are continually driving one another on in the way to ruin.

Sin when it is finished brings forth complete and remediless moral ruin in the individual, and transforms the society of transgressors into hell. There is no reason for believing that there is any other kind of hell than that which is thus produced. Such a hell would be deep enough and hot enough to answer all the demands of the most strenuous orthodoxy.

From this condition of spiritual death the Lord of Life seeks to deliver men. It was because the gravitations of sin are so deadly that He came, not to set aside the law by which sin brings death, but to give men power to resist its downward pull, and to rise into moral health and newness of life.

The work which He does for us is described in the New Testament by a great variety of phrases, some of which are boldly imaginative, but all of which can be understood if we keep in mind the end He had in view, the saving of His people from their sins.

It is said by one apostle that He "was made sin for us, though He knew no sin, that we might become the righteousness of God in Him" (2 Cor. v. 21). It is not necessary to interpret this, as Luther and many others have done, as meaning that Jesus actually became a sinner. Its full meaning is sufficiently set forth if we take it as expressing the complete identification of Christ with humanity.

He is said by another apostle to have borne our sins in His own body on the tree (1 Peter ii. 24). We need not understand this as teaching that our sins were imputed to Him, but simply that the sufferings which He endured upon the cross were inflicted on Him by human sin. It was the jealousy and madness of men that caused Him to suffer. Every taunt, every blow, was a direct manifestation of human sin. It is not in any forensic sense, but in a sense perfectly literal, that He "bore our sins in His own body on the tree."

He is also said to have "redeemed us from the curse of the law, being made a curse for us" (Gal. iii. 13). What is the curse of the law? It is the corporate wickedness and the corporate woe of the world. It is the spiritual death whose dire work we have traced in the individual and in society. It is seen nowhere in its complete results, for the redeeming grace of God is everywhere at work repairing its ruins and checking its worst tendencies, but we see enough of it to be able to form some conception of what it would be but for this redeeming and restraining grace. This inbred evil, working itself out everywhere in deceit and corruption and cruelty, is the curse of the law. The penalty of sin is sin. The curse that falls on a man when he transgresses is the strengthening of sin in him and the lessening of his desire and his power to escape from it. He that sows to the flesh reaps corruption. The society composed of such individuals sinks, as we have seen, by the same law. Evil men and seducers wax worse and worse, deceiving and being deceived. "Iniquity unto iniquity," sin upon sin, shame upon shame, hate upon hate, a swift progression downward—this is the curse of the law. The sin and moral disorder of the world to-day are, therefore, not only a cause but a consequence. They are the harvest of the iniquity of former offences. All this ingrained and organic wickedness, the falsehood and impurity, and selfishness and spite and malice of the world, are the curse of sin. Jesus bore the curse. He came into the scene of moral disorder and madness and exposed Himself to all its evil. He sought no exemption from the common lot; He confronted all this violence and hatred as men must, and suffered as men do, and as much more than men suffer as His nature was more sensitive than that of the best of us. The work that He sought to do He could not do unless He became one with us, encountering all the dire consequences of the world's evil—enduring, if you choose so to express it, the penalty of the world's sin. Thus it is that Christ bore the curse for us that He might redeem us from the curse of the law.

It is also said that He magnified the law and made it honourable (Isaiah xlii. 21). These words of Isaiah have no reference to Christ, but they may be applied to Him. For by the suffering which He endured He honoured the law of God. The law under which suffering comes upon the race as the result of sin is a good and righteous law. The curse of the law is a righteous retribution. The sin in which we are all involved ought to bring to us all trouble and misery. The solidarity of the race is a mighty fact; all the good we hope for is bound up with it, and we cannot have the good which it brings without exposing ourselves to the evil which it entails. When Jesus refused to set aside this law on His own behalf, He honoured the law by a most impressive testimony.

Not only by enduring its penalty, but by perfectly obeying its precept He magnified the law; and still more gloriously has He honoured it by leading millions who were once disobeying it to love it and keep it.

Such interpretations may give us the deeper spiritual meaning contained in the phrases which tell us that He "bore our sins in His own body on the tree"; that "He suffered the curse of the law, being made a curse for us";

that "He magnified the law and made it honourable."

His Atonement is the reconciliation of man to God, and the method of reconciliation is revelation. He revealed man to Himself, and He revealed God to man.

By His sufferings He revealed men to Himself. It was human bigotry and envy that crucified Him. Thus the death of Christ revealed to man the depth of sin in his own heart as it had never before been revealed. The fact that perfect goodness in His person was hated and scorned and crucified by men is an object-lesson by which the pride of man in all ages has been humbled.

Not only in His sufferings, but also in His whole life, He reveals God to men. In Him, says the beloved apostle, the life of God was manifested. In His humility and gentleness, in His lowly service, in His works of healing, in His sympathy with the sorrowful, in His friendship for the despised and the degraded, He reveals to men that God whom He has taught us to call Our Father. At the end of this life of self-denying service, while all these gracious ministries were fresh in the minds of His disciples, one of them said to Him, "Show us the Father and it sufficeth us. Jesus said unto him, Have I been so long time with you, and yet hast thou not known Me, Philip? He that hath seen Me hath seen the Father." How should we be able rightly to interpret the saying that God is Love if we had not the record of the life of Jesus Christ? God loved the world, but how and how much? We must needs go back to the Gospels and read their record. And when we have studied again the life of Him who went about doing good; when we have brought again to our remembrance the truth that this lowly Servant and Sufferer was one who could say, "I and My Father are one"; when we have witnessed again the mighty love of One whose feet never rested on their errands of mercy, and the heroic patience of Him who endured such contradiction of sinners against Himself, dying at last a victim of their spite, and conquering their enmity by enduring its deadliest assault—then we are able to put some meaning into those wonderful words, and to say, "God *so* loved the world," "herein is Love." And it is by this revelation that God has reconciled the world unto Himself, subduing the enmity. It is this great revelation of God's forgiveness which moves us to seek and accept His grace of forgiveness.

"And if," says the apostle, "while we were enemies we were reconciled to God by the death of His Son, much more, being reconciled, we shall be saved by His life." Alienation from God results in spiritual death, reconciliation with Him is the return to the soul of spiritual life. The branch that was cut off and was withering is reunited to the vine and lives again in the life of the vine. That loving fellowship with the Highest into which the revelation of God in Christ leads us restores the soul; we are made partakers of the Divine nature; the law of the spirit of life in Christ Jesus makes us free from the law of sin and death; we receive of His fulness and grace upon grace, each gift making room for a larger gift. The natural consequences of sin are counteracted, and the ruin of sin is repaired by the restorative and remedial power of the Divine life, thus communicated to the soul.

The soul that is thus reunited to God by faith is by love made one with its fellow men. We cannot, in any true sense, return to the Father without entering into His thoughts concerning our brethren. As the sin that separates us from God weakens the social bond and gives us on earth the substance of hell, so the love that brings us back to God restores the social bond and gives us on earth the substance of heaven.

All attempts to set forth in reasoned, philosophic phrases the nature of that saving work of Christ for which the Christian believer gives thanks to God must needs be fragmentary and inadequate. How incomplete this statement is no one knows better than he who has made it. One can say but little, after all, about the things that mean most to him—the majesty of mountains, the glory of the sky; how much less can the whole content of Incarnation and

Redemption be set forth in any mere logical forms! Yet such attempts must needs be made, and it may be that by means of these imperfect words some troubled minds may be able to gain new glimpses of that Mystery of Godliness into which the angels desire to look.

XII.

BY ALFRED CAVE, B.A., D.D
Principal of Hackney College

Upon what conditions can God forgive sin? Concerning one condition all are agreed—the repentance of the sinner. And repentance is the only condition, it has sometimes, if rarely, been said; "the doctrine of Scripture is that of free forgiveness." If such be the case, a method of rule is supposed to answer in the universe which does not succeed in any home, or society, or nation. What further condition is there, then, of the Divine forgiveness of sins? The atoning death of Jesus is the remarkable reply of Scripture. This atoning death we are to strive to understand.

Presently I shall dare to enter upon the eminently venturous task of framing a theory of the Atonement, but before doing so I think it desirable to say a few words concerning a common misapprehension.

A theory of the Atonement, it seems to me, plays very little part in the evangelistic work of the Churches. Belief in the saving work of Christ is of two kinds. There is an assurance born of experience, and a conviction born of prolonged thought. On the one hand, many hold most firmly to the saving influence of Jesus who have never studied with any care the intellectual evidence for that saving influence. Perhaps constitution, or possibly circumstance, precludes them from collecting or weighing the related facts. But a man need not be a theologian to be saved. Without holding any formal theory of the Atonement, a man may rejoice in salvation by the death of Jesus. The Christian's consciousness of the forgiveness of sins through the Cross of Christ is one of the most distinct of all spiritual intuitions, and is open to all. Nor, though unreasoned, is this experimental belief irrational. Such initial knowledge is sure, if inchoate, and precious, though inexpressible. Not by an intellectual grasp of a theory of Atonement is it produced, but by the direct testimony of the Holy Ghost. The Holy Spirit uses some word of a preacher, or some verse of a hymn, or some story of experience, or some Scripture phrase or passage, and, working thereupon, brings sight to the blind, or resurrection to the dead, or Gospel to the poor. In the innermost realms of soul, by the power of the Holy Spirit, an indelible assurance is born that Christ's death has become our life. In a word, there is a belief in the saving power of the death of Christ which is the product of faith.

Nevertheless, a theory of the Atonement, it also seems to me, is of great force in the production of a robust Christianity. It is a useful part of the intellectual and moral education of the Christian. If there is a religious assurance concerning the Atonement open to all, there is a theological conviction thereupon open to all who will think. It is possible to argue as well as state our convictions concerning our salvation, to weigh all the related facts, to express their exact tenour. It is possible to give many a reason for the faith that is in us, drawn, it may be, from the pages of Scripture, or the facts of experience, or the stores of history, or the results of reasoning. Now this belief, which is the product of the Christian intellect, has a great staying power. It guides in personal or pastoral perplexity. It imparts a maturer air to the teacher and preacher. It has pleasures of its own to bestow, and healthiness and support. Theological conviction when arrived at has the ripeness of an ultimate certainty.

To a man conscious of sin and anxious for forgiveness, I should not present a carefully thought-out theory of the Atonement, I should present Christ—the dying Christ, the everliving Christ—as the Gospels or as personal experience have taught me. The living Christ, I should trust, would, by the Spirit He sends, demonstrate the saving power of His death. Happily, entrance into the Kingdom of God is not by examination in the theory of the Atonement. Entrance is by practical ways, not intellectual—by following Christ; that is, by striving, with effort and prayer and self-denial, to feel with Jesus and act with Jesus and think with Jesus. But the maturer follower of Christ, in his prolonged struggle to think, as well as to feel and act with Jesus, will find a theory of the Atonement of incalculable value, strengthening his own belief and imparting the expert touch in dealing with souls.

Passing to the theory of the Atonement, any adequate theory, be it remembered, must (1) explain without strain all the Scriptural references to the Atonement—its nature, its necessity, its objects, its effects; (2) must also emphasize or correct all the various lessons taught in the course of the thought of centuries; and (3) must at the same time respect the suggestions of the Christian consciousness, and especially of the Christianised moral sense. No theory can be considered adequate which does not take note of all the facts, the teaching of the Bible and of Christian experience and of the history of Christian doctrine, the demands of the heart and of the intellect and of the conscience.

Once, in this series of papers, it has been said that the Biblical revelation upon the Atonement cannot be expressed "in systematically logical form, because it is presented in varying metaphors." There cannot be a theory of the Atonement, it has been said, because there is no unity in the mode of representation. The Biblical points of view are certainly numerous. According to the Scriptures Christ died to obtain eternal life for man *(John* iii. 15); to secure the gift of the Spirit *(Gal.* iii. 13, 14); to purchase the forgiveness of sin *(Ephes.* i. 7); to abolish sin *(Heb.* ix. 26); to reconcile us to God *(Col.* i. 19, 20); to justify us *(Rom.* iii. 24, 26); to sanctify us *(Heb.* xiii. 12); to redeem us from selfishness *(2 Cor.* v. 15). Again, by the death of Jesus we are told the love of God was manifested *(Rom.* v. 8) and His holiness *(Rom.* iii. 25, 26), the obedience of Christ was declared *(John* vi. 38), and His heroism *(1 Pet.* ii. 21, 23), Satan was defeated *(Col.* ii. 13-15) a ransom was paid *(Matt.* xx. 28), a sacrifice was offered *(Heb.* x. 14), an atonement was made *(1 John* ii. 2). Yet again, in other forms of speech, it is said that the death of Jesus was the death of a surety *(Heb.* vii. 22), of a substitute *(Gal.* iii. 13), and of a representative *(Heb.* ii. 16, 17). Yet again, according to the Bible, the necessity for atonement is to be found in the sin of man *(Heb.* ix. 26*)*, in the holiness of God *(Rom.* iii. 25, 26*)*, in the love of God *(*1 *John* ix. 10*)*, in the relationship of Christ to God and to man *(Col.* i. 14-18*)*, in the love of Jesus for man *(Gal.* ii. 20*)*. And yet again, the death of Jesus is described in the New Testament as voluntary *(John* x. 17, 18*)*, as obedient *(Rom.* v. 19), as altruistic *(Heb.* ii. 9*)*, as vicarious *(Matt.* xx. 28*)*, as a sinless death *(*2 *Cor.* v. 21*)*, as a suffering death *(*1 *Pet.* iii. 18*)*, as a sacrificial death *(Ephes.* v. 2*)*, as the death of the God-Man *(Phil.* ii. 6-8*)*. Certainly the Biblical points of view are diverse, very diverse. But the question is not their diversity, but their possible unity. Is it possible to bring all these variant points of view under one consistent theory? I believe it is.

But it is not surprising that a satisfactory theory was long in coming. Nor is it wonderful that crude theories of many kinds preceded more satisfactory theories. Such is the way in matters of human thinking. It took the thought of a thousand years even to realise all the conditions of the problem. For centuries attempts were made to explain all the Biblical references to Atonement by the idea of ransom. And for centuries after, some single Biblical metaphor was pushed to unwarrantable extremes. The story may be read in several good books. Eventually two great theories, in many forms, developed themselves, each passing through a remarkable and interesting evolution from crudeness to delicacy, and from narrowness to breadth. These two theories are respectively known as the Moral Theory and the Substitutionary Theory. According to the Moral theory, not a self-interpreting name, the death of Jesus is an atonement addressed by God to man, and reconciling, as the phrase goes, man to God. According to the Substitutionary theory, again neither a self-explanatory nor good name, the death of Christ is an Atonement addressed by man to God, reconciling, as the phrase goes, both God to man and man to God.

It is a form of the so-called Substitutionary theory which has appealed to me with ever more clearness and force, since the conditions of the problem became evident to me, and since I first began to write upon the question, now more than twenty years ago. Those conditions it may be desirable to tabulate sharply, as far as I understand them. Thus, in the first place, any theory of the Atonement which would solve all the phases of the problem must not contradict any of the Biblical points of view. Secondly, it must harmonise with the other great doctrines of Scripture, of God and the Trinity, of man and his Divine origin, of sin and its awful consequences, of Salvation and its pressing necessity. Thirdly, the theory must not repeat those theories which time has shown to be inadequate. Fourthly, the theory must give due weight to all the positions which time has made more and more credible. Fifthly, the theory must not contradict the intuitions of the moral sense; for instance, there must be no talk of the transfer of sin or guilt from the sinner to the Saviour (neither punishment nor repentance can be vicarious), or talk of the cancelling of the sinner's sin by the suffering of the Saviour (the sinner must bear his own penalty), or talk of God the Father being full of vengeance which fell upon the Son (God is love), or of Christ paying the very same penalty, or an equivalent penalty, to that due to all the sins of those whom He saves (for if some only are saved the Atonement is limited and not universal, and if all are saved, salvation is universal and compulsory). The theory which has most commended itself to me, as answering all these conditions, is a maturer form of the theory, first crudely stated by Duns Scotus, a little less crudely stated by Grotius, more cautiously stated by the earlier New England theologians, and most commonly held by writers upon the Atonement amongst the Nonconformists of England and the Protestants of Germany, and France; the theory, too, advocated in the Congregational lectures of Gilbert and Dale.

I should state the theory somewhat as follows, simply indicating, however, the salient points:—

Created in the image of God—with a spiritual nature, that is—and therefore intelligent, free and accountable, man's destiny was to grow ever more into the Divine likeness. Man—flesh and spirit, innocent, sane in frame and mind though inexperienced as a babe—was to become holy, undying, cultured on all sides of his nature, ever growing, from father to son, and from age to age, towards a more perfect stature. The main condition of this human progress was continuous communion with God. God is life, and with God is life. God with man is the condition of all healthy and genuine progress.

When sin intervened, the very essence of sin being man's withdrawal from God, sin involved death. According to the law of the universe, sin is followed by death. Man who "lives" with God, "dies" without Him.

But the consequences of sin should be put more explicitly. They are twofold, and are as sure as any physical law. Sin affected man and sin affected God. Man himself breaks the fellowship between himself and God, with results upon both himself and God. On the one hand normal development is interrupted. The same influences for good and growth no longer stream forth upon man. Sin works death. Man dies. The gigantic evolution of living without God, with its various phases (which is death), has commenced. And man is part of a series. One generation influences the generation following. As a righteous race would produce a race with a predisposition to righteousness, a sinful race produces a race with a predisposition to sin. On the other hand, sin, the rejection of God, produces another class of effects. God becomes morally estranged. In Scriptural language, the "wrath" of God breaks forth. Wrath is righteous indignation; it is energetic holiness; it is the pure anger of the King of all worlds at the intrusion of sin into His holy dominion. If sin produces, by natural consequence, "death" in man, it is because sin has first evoked "wrath" in God.

Consider, therefore, the twofold conditions of salvation from sin. If the ravage of sin is to be stayed, and man is to be rescued one thing is clear. Means must be found to neutralise moral corruption, and to reintroduce "life" where "death" reigns. Evidently the depraving effects of sin upon man may be conquered by regeneration. God with us again means life eternal. By restored vital union with God, by the life in us of the Holy Ghost, we may be saved, and our children after us, from the corruption which is in the world through lust. This side of the question is simple enough. Corruption may be mastered by regeneration. But there is another side. How shall the schism in the universe because of sin be healed? How shall the moral disaster in the sphere of holy government be rectified? Here comes in the gracious Gospel of God. As experience shows, and as careful survey accentuates, the holy wrath of God is met by the atoning death of Jesus, His only Son.

But how can such a death atone? This is the crux of the whole. The awful consequences of sin are the laws of God, instituted, as we must believe and can see, for the good of the universe. They are the ordering of His holy will in view of the interests of all worlds. Sin must lead to death, and so itself die out, says the Infinite Father and Holy Ruler. The universe would ultimately be freed from sin by the very law of sin, by the death of every sinner. But is the death of every sinner the only way of terminating sin? How can the death of Jesus break the awful chain of cause and effect, of sin and death?

Does not the answer come from the aim of punishment? Punishment is a necessity of holy rule. The arm of the law is inseparable from righteous government. But why? Surely to secure righteous rule in the interests of all, and to secure righteous rule by vindicating righteousness. As a matter of fact, the death of Jesus is a more splendid vindication of righteous rule than the death of all sinners would be. He who, for the good of the entire universe, made the law that death should follow sin, from love of the whole universe submits His sinless self to death. Who could say thenceforth, whether man or devil, that sin had been lightly forgiven and the interests of holy rule endangered? By His death as man, and all its inexplicable suffering, the God-Man made it possible to restore His life as God to any sinners willing to avail themselves thereof. Man may become regenerate if he will, not alone because Christ died, the just for the unjust, but because Christ ever lives, having "the keys of death and Hades." By dying the God-Man demonstrated that He who made the universe and its laws does not lightly esteem His own righteous nature and rule and man's truest good therein, but will rather Himself suffer for man's sake and God's. As the heart feels instinctively and the intellect knows after thought, such a death suffices to open the way for all who repent to the regenerating life of God. By such a sacrifice moral law is more vindicated than by the death of every sinner, whilst, by so unexpected but so stupendous a display of compassion, the Divine love touches our hearts acutely. Glory be to God, Father and Son and Spirit.

On such a theory all the Bible statements

previously summarised and all the truth in the history of doctrine receive fitting place and explanation. By His death Jesus destroyed the empire of Satan. Anselm's false idea of honour as seen in chivalry, is rectified by the truer idea of honour as due to holy government. In the light of such a theory we see why Christ is the High Priest, and sacrifice, and offering for sin. Upon such a theory all the Old Testament figures fall into lucid place We see why the death of Jesus was a *satisfaction* (satisfaction having reference to the claims of law), and a *reconciliation* (which has reference to estrangement), and an *expiation* (which has reference to sin), and a *propitiation* (which has reference to wrath).

XIII.

BY BERNARD J. SNELL, M.A., B.Sc.

"Our Father who art in heaven, hallowed be Thy Name."

THE religions of the old world were bound up with sacrifices. Men trembled before God. All the misfortunes which came upon them they deemed the visitation of the wrath of Heaven, and by bloody offerings they sought to gratify their deities and to make amends for transgressions. Whatever may be the correct philosophic explanation of this fact, such was the fact, the universal fact.

Our Lord's teaching was revolutionary. He unveiled the love of the Father, and thereby for ever extinguished the ancient error. He bade men believe that with grave misunderstanding they had entirely misconceived the Almighty. The priests had been wrong, the prophets had been right. "God spake not unto your fathers nor commanded them concerning burnt offerings or sacrifices." "Did ye offer unto Me sacrifices and gifts in the wilderness for forty years, O House of Israel?" "When ye come to appear before Me, who hath required this at your hands?" Sacrifice (says Dr. G. A. Smith) has never been the Divine, the revealed element in the religion of Jehovah. Spiritual prophecy assigned not the slightest value to sacrifices; all the prophets from Amos to Jeremiah denounced the sacrificial system. Divine favour and forgiveness are the immediate consequence of repentance of sin. Penitence is as sure of pardon, as sin is sure of punishment. God delights to forgive; He needs no urging to it. Nothing is more central to the Gospel of Christ than this —that the redeeming mercy of God is spontaneous, not prompted or purchased. "God becomes the Saviour by the ethical necessities of His nature."

Most of the theories of Atonement appear to me to have sprung from the age-long endeavour to graft the Revelation of Jesus Christ on to the old-world error of sacrificialism. In that futile attempt men have been driven to say things dreadfully dishallowing to the Father's Name, and to shape concerning the death of Christ doctrines which contradict the teaching of Christ.

In the early Christians this was more pardonable than it is in us. They had been accustomed to the sacrificial system; it was integral with their thought, their feeling, their language. They could not suddenly cut themselves adrift from all their past. Our Lord's teaching bewildered them; they could receive the new truth only in the modes of thought natural to them. When they tried to express the truth of Christ, they employed terms borrowed from the old mistake, terms which for us only obscure the simplicity that was in Christ. It was in that *milieu* that the old doctrine of Atonement crystallised, in minds wherein Hebraic and Pagan ideas persisted. We make a mistake if we take their symbols of thought as equivalents of spiritual realities, of if we treat their sentences as propositions from which we may deduce the uttermost corollaries. Their figures are illustrative, not definitive; their expressions were forced on them by their past thought and experience, and are flung out towards truth as their best means of approximating to it.

Let me put it still more plainly. They had lost their Lord: He had been vilely slain. They had been used to offer sacrifices, they now knew from Jesus that they needed to sacrifice no more. Was any thought more inevitable to their minds than this—that Christ had been the all-satisfying victim, and that everything which legal sacrifices and ceremonial observances had effected the Saviour's death had wrought for all for ever? So was framed the theory of His propitiatory sacrifice, a theory which no subtilty can co-ordinate with our Lord's teaching or with the honour which is due to the Holy Father ever hallowed.

But that theory survives. Luther said, "God's anger against the sinner was so fierce that He could be appeased only by the blood of His Son"; and Article II. of the Church of England lays it down that "Christ was crucified to reconcile His Father to us and to be a sacrifice." (The meaning of the words is so unmistakable that no sophistication can blunt their edge.) But if Christ became our Saviour by appeasing an angry god, then He first saved that god; such a theory ruins the character of the god whose action it sets forth. A god whose anger must be appeased by the blood of the innocent is a god whom to worship were infamous.

There is an occasional attempt made to lessen the ghastliness of this appalling doctrine by saying that our Lord's death was needed, not to appease God's wrath, but to satisfy His justice. He was willing, even anxious, to forgive men, but it was not safe for Him to do so until adequate penalty was paid for sin. He could not remit the penalty to the penitent offender, but was willing to transfer it to an innocent substitute. As if justice did not care by whom the pain was suffered, so that it was suffered! As if the integrity of the Divine Government could be vindicated only by the punishment of the innocent! As if in a God-governed world an unjust act was necessary before mercy could season justice! We dare not admit such an idea into our moral nature; we dare not assign such a principle of action to the Father.

Nor let us confuse ourselves by saying, "It is above reason, but not contrary to reason." That is an unintelligible phrase, to which we can attach no meaning. By that door enters superstition.

Let us go back to the plain teaching of Jesus. Therein is the corrective to all false doctrine. Our Lord never said or suggested that the Divine forgiveness waited on His suffering the death of the Cross. He never represented the Father as unable or unready to receive a repentant prodigal, or as requiring to know that something had been done in addition to repentance, or as demanding that somebody else suffered before He was justified in forgiving. Dare any of us say that a soul filled with sorrow for sin can remain unpardoned of God?

"But the parable of the prodigal does not

contain all the truth!" No; but in that parable Jesus was explicitly showing the Divine method of recovery. And that is the subject in question. I do not read in that story any shadowed hint that God would need a suspension of the moral laws of the universe in order to forgive; to me it seems as if His forgiveness were the most natural thing in the world. "Forgive us our trespasses, as we forgive them that trespass against us." That is straightforward and comprehensible enough. No cataclysm is necessary to enable God to forgive His repentant children; nay, rather miracle were needed to *prevent* God from pardoning the penitent. The whole difficulty is not in inducing or enabling God to pardon, but in moving men to abhor sin and to want pardon. We ought not to impeach the moral government of God by presenting Christ's death as an expedient introduced in order to render it possible for God to forgive sinners. It was no expedient; it was a manifestation of the grace of God which eternally abounds. It was not a mechanical device, it was a moral appeal, a revelation of God to heart and mind and conscience.

And some will say, "You are making the death of Christ less than the teaching of Christ." I do nothing of the kind. By this way of looking at it the message of the death of Christ is made congruous with the teaching of Christ. And I venture to add that if my reader is a Christian in any real sense he has no right to frame a theory of the death of Christ which is contradicted throughout by the plain teaching of Christ again and again repeated. His teaching is simple, inescapable, undeniable; your theories of Atonement are hopelessly confused and contradictory. Unless your theory accords with Christ's teaching it stands condemned. No amount of argument can alter the plain fact that Christ taught us that it is God's strong and passionate desire to find His children and to make them one with Himself for ever. The emphasis of His Gospel lies there—in the redeeming love of God—and to that He sealed His witness by His death.

And some will say, "We agree that what Christ said is most true, but after all something more is essential to the Gospel than is found in Christ's teaching." As if our Lord did not preach the whole Gospel of Christ! Surely he must be a bold man who declares that they who heard Christ preach are to be numbered among those to whom the Gospel was not preached. The Gospel did not begin to be in A.D 33. Christianity was a revelation, not a creation. Would there have been no Gospel had not Christ died? Were His teachings defective until they were expanded and supplemented by the teachings of St. Paul and St. Augustine? I am aware that Dr. Dale said (Biography, 665): "I find in the Epistles to the Romans and Ephesians a fuller manifestation of the mind of Christ than in the Sermon on the Mount." With all deference to so fearless a champion of Christian truth, I shrink from such an assertion more than I care to tell, and regard it as expressive of the straits to which frank exponents of the old theory were driven. Christ less evangelical than Paul!

Surely nothing perpetrated by the most daring of "higher critics" is comparable with that. Surely He who said, "One is your Teacher and all ye are brethren," claimed for Himself as a Teacher something more than is accorded to Him on this theory.

Why, then, did Christ die? Why must the Son of Man needs suffer? Not to create a new fact in God, but to create a new fact in us; not to change the disposition of God toward men, but to change the disposition of men toward God; not (as the Article says) to reconcile God to us, but to reconcile us to God. Only by dying for the sheep could the Shepherd make the sheep understand His love; only by being "lifted up" could He draw all men unto Him. Am I not right when I say that this was our Lord's way of regarding His death? "I, if I be lifted up from the earth, will draw all men unto Me." Therefore, that He might bring His children home to His feet, "God spared not His own Son, but delivered Him up for us all."

Saith Thomas à Kempis, "When Thou, O

my God, wouldst show Thy love for the world, Thou gavest it Thy Son. When Thou wouldst show Thy love for Thy Son, Thou gavest Him a cross." And while He hung in death, men said, " If Thou be the Son of God, come down from the cross," not discerning that it was because He was the Son of God that He was on the cross.

> Through the shadow of an agony
> Cometh Redemption.

There is a Divine appeal in suffering, an appeal that needs no argument and is susceptible of no explanation. The early Moravian missionaries in Greenland laboured for long years in the inculcation of principles of truth and right, and laboured fruitlessly, but when one of them read the story of our Saviour's death, his hearers exclaimed, "Why did you not tell us this before? Tell us it again." Nothing lies so close to the hearts of His own as do our Lord's sufferings.

> Pre-eminent in one thing most of all
> The Man of Sorrows; and the Cross of Christ
> Is more to us than all His miracles.

Was it necessary? In the world we know—

Yes. Necessary, not because the Divine nature is what it is, but because human nature is what it is. In the world we know, unless Christ had suffered, we should never have gained, I say not an adequate, but an approximate, idea of His devotion and love. *That* was the culmination of His lifelong obedience, the supreme proof of His fidelity to the Father. *So* He finished the work which was given Him to do—the manifestation of the love of God; so He became the Mediator, perfect through sufferings. Doing the will of God *to the end* He made the complete sacrifice. His Cross was the climax of a lifelong sacrifice, and in the light that streams from it Christ's Gospel is glorified.

In the world we know He would have been the world's greatest religious teacher, without that final passion; but He would not have become the world's Saviour. Men did not believe in the love of God until the Holy One died for the love of God. The death of Jesus was the life of the world. In that sign Christ conquered the human heart, and stands for ever in the glory of the Father.

Thou must love Me who have died for thee.

And I believe that "God was in Christ reconciling the world unto Himself," and that "God hath shined in our hearts to give the light of the knowledge of the glory of God in the face of Jesus Christ."

XIV.

BY C. SILVESTER HORNE, M.A.

THERE is no doctrine that has its roots more clearly in the Old Testament than the doctrine of Atonement. It is a matter of great surprise to many that in some of the best-known treatises on the doctrine little or nothing is said about the place of Atonement in the Old Testament. Yet much crude and dangerous statement of the theory has arisen from pressing unduly the rough types and figures of speech which Old Testament ritual set forth for the instruction of a race in the religious childhood of the world. It is quite true, doubtless, that

> Truth embodied in a tale,
> May enter in at lowly doors.

But there is always the danger that a good deal that is not truth may enter in with it. It is well to begin by recognising that acts of atonement belong to the religious history of man. They are not even characteristically Jewish or

Christian. They belong to the religious history of man; and the form of their expression is almost or quite universally in sacrifices. To analyse the motives that inspired even the rudest and most repulsive sacrifices is probably to do them injustice. Higher and lower motives, as we all know, mingle frequently in our most religious actions; and even where terror has been the ruling motive in sacrifice we need not dispute that there has often been a holier form of fear and respect. It is worth while to take clear note that alike in heathenism and paganism men have groped their way to a position which has promise of the highest in it—that for a man to make his peace with God he must be prepared to offer God his best. He must be willing to make any and every sacrifice. Tennyson gave us powerful representation of that in "The Victim." The plague was destroying the people, when

> The priest in horror about his altar
> To Thor and Odin lifted his hand:
> "Help us from famine
> And plague and strife.
> What would you have of us?

> Human life?
> Were it our nearest,
> Were it our dearest,
> (Answer, oh, answer!)
> We give you his life."

Here is the root idea of propitiation through acts of atonement; a people making its peace with God—or, more accurately, seeking to make God at peace with it—through the sacrifice of what is highest and dearest. That is what we mean when we say that acts of atonement belong to the religious history of man.

Just here, however, a distinction emerges. Such acts of atonement are not in all cases connected with any sense of sin. Heathen and Pagan deities were very arbitrary beings, moved by very human passions. They were spiteful, malicious, envious, mischievous. Because they chose to persecute some race or tribe, it did not follow that the people had done anything to deserve it. It was policy on the part of the people to placate this persecuting deity; but the persecution did not connect itself with the consciousness of any moral defect in themselves. After all, it was the Hebrew religion, with its magnificent emphasis of the moral nature, that first definitely associated sacrifice and sin; that fully recognised that that which moves the wrath of God is wickedness; and that Atonement—Peace with God—must be sought through sacrifice, because of a broken law and the condemnation that rests upon the man who breaks it.

To confirm this, let me mention a further point. The Heathen or Pagan deed of propitiation was done when some special emergency demanded it. If all went smoothly and prosperously there was no act of atonement. The gods were assumed to be at peace with men; and men had no inner conviction of sin prompting them to seek God's mercy. But the Hebrew had his solemn season of atonement *every year;* for whether the national fortunes were good or bad, he knew that there was need to entreat the mercy of God for a cleansing from sin. All the people were made to recognise in this way that their sins ever demanded the mercy of God to cover them, and their hearts the power of God to cleanse them from the taint and stain of moral guilt.

It is of interest and importance to note with care the leading features of the Day of Atonement, so that we may carry to our discussion of the Christian doctrine the various Hebrew conceptions which entered so largely into the thought of Paul and of the author of the Epistle to the Hebrews. Let us examine this impressive ritual point by point.

1. The act of atonement was the work of one man—the High Priest. The High Priest was never so solitary a figure in the life of Israel as on the Day of Atonement and the days immediately preceding it. He stood absolutely and awfully alone. His office was then, most of all, that of a mediator—to confess the sins of the people to God and to affirm the mercy of God to the people. For this work he was separated from all men, even his own household, for seven days. He was not to come in contact with any form of evil, or death, or

sin, lest he should contract pollution. For the sake of the work of atonement he must be " separate from sinners."

2. Let us observe the work of the High Priest. After performing the ordinary rites of the day in his ordinary coloured robes, he begins the special rites by assuming the white robe. This is the emblem, of course, of absolute personal purity in the Mediator. He is to do what can only be done by one perfect in innocency.

3. In connection with the sacrifices there was a certain notable order. First, a sacrifice for the priest and his household; secondly, for the sanctuary and all contained in it; and thirdly, for the people. A pure ministry, a pure church, a pure people.

4. To make atonement he entered into the Holy of Holies. The impression on the mind of the people was that the supreme act of atonement required some special approach to the Divine Presence. It was an act involving a certain awful familiarity and intimacy with God. The atoning Person must come forth

from the immediate Presence to reveal a redeeming grace.

5. The sacrifice for the people was notable. Out of the public treasury, as signifying that every person had share and lot in the transaction, two goats were purchased. These two were presented at the door of the Tabernacle, and lots were cast. Two pieces of boxwood were put into an urn, one of which was marked " for Jehovah," and the other "for Azazel." When the lot had been cast, the goat marked for Jehovah was slain and its blood sprinkled before the mercy-seat in token of Penitence depending upon Mercy. Then the High Priest laid his hands upon the head of the goat marked for Azazel, and confessed over it the sins of the people. This goat was then led away "into uninhabited places." The meaning of Azazel is disputed; but the symbolic intent of the rite is clear. It was a sacrifice made sin for the people; enduring, as the awful penalty of sin, exile, alienation, estrangement. Its absolute disappearance, too, was to indicate that as far as the east is from the

west so far hath God removed transgressions from the people.

Such was the Day of Atonement. But one more fact remains to be noted. A certain moral condition attached to participation in its privileges. The people were commanded "to afflict themselves," and to rest from worldly occupations. This was surely to imply that all the work of the High Priest would not avail for them apart from a certain moral preparedness. The Jews had, in point of fact, innumerable rites for putting away a sin. But this Day of Atonement assumed a sinful nature, and habits of sin which could not be atoned for by occasional penances. Finally, we note that it was Atonement for a race, or a whole people. I have said that its efficacy for the individual depended upon his personal attitude towards the act. But the act was done, not for one or two, but for all the people. Men are strangely knit together by virtue of a common sinful nature; and there is an act of atonement for all of them.

Now all these points are seen to have great

interest and importance when we turn to the doctrine of Atonement in the New Testament. It comes, indeed, to many persons as a surprise to discover that the word atonement does not occur in the New Testament. Once it appeared in the old version, though it is impossible to say why. The word so translated is simply the word reconciliation, and the word atonement is used in its philological sense of at-one-ment. It is a reconciling or bringing together of two existences which have become estranged. This is, of course, always the root idea of atonement. The awful effect of sin is to separate, alienate the soul from God. Christ's work, we are all agreed, is to bring men to God; and He does it by saving them from their sins.

It will be well to dismiss, very emphatically, certain ideas which are quite unscriptural and ought to have no place in any theology. Old statements of the doctrine of atonement left the impression, especially on young minds, that God the Father was always angry with us, and waiting to punish us; but Jesus sought to appease His Father's wrath, took our side,

pleaded our cause, and when God's anger could
be stayed in no other way, presented Himself to
the rod of the Smiter, and the punishment
which should have fallen on us fell on Him. So
He died, the just for the unjust, that He might
bring us to God. Suffice it to say, that there is
no such antagonism between justice in God and
mercy in Christ anywhere in the New Testament. The supreme end and purpose of
Christ's mission and work was to incite mankind to faith in the infinite love and grace of
our Father-God, which our sins have made it so
difficult for us to believe in.

Take another common supposition. It used
to be more the custom than it is now to dwell
in great detail on the physical agonies endured
by Jesus. It was implied, and indeed asserted,
that these sufferings were laid upon the Holy
Son by the Father so that we, the unholy,
might not have to bear them. It is absolutely
imperative that we should be clear in our
minds that the vital and effectual factor in
the Atonement is not the sufferings of
Christ, but the love and holiness of Christ. All

that He endured He voluntarily endured because of the so great love wherewith He loved us. There is no possible clue to His Life-and-Death mystery but this—God so loved that He suffered; God so loved that He gave; gave, as Christ said, His life a ransom for many.

Just one more common but groundless supposition. It is nowhere said in the New Testament that God *punished* Christ. It is nowhere said that Christ voluntarily endured punishment at His Father's hands instead of us. This was the crude presentation of certain facts we must look at later.

> He knew how wicked man had been,
> He knew that God must punish sin,
> So, out of pity, Jesus said
> He'd bear the punishment instead.

There is this false idea of a Father, who must punish out of justice, punishing an innocent Son instead of the guilty ones, because that innocent Son was so pitiful that He interposed Himself between the wrath and the sin that had deserved the wrath. The justice is with God; the mercy is with Jesus; and in the thought of most people to-day, the justice becomes injustice because innocence suffers while guilt escapes scot free.

And now, in our examination of New Testament teaching, we shall find that it groups itself around certain leading words—Propitiation, Reconciliation, Redemption and a fourth class of words represented by the preposition "for"—*For* us, *For* our sins.

1. *Propitiation.*—This will not detain us long; but it must detain us long enough for us to disabuse our minds of any idea that the old Pagan conception has any place in Christianity. Jesus Christ is not offered to propitiate God. Jesus is represented as God's own offering to propitiate man and win back to God the alienated heart, lost in the love of self and sin.

This is easily seen, because the passages where the word occurs are few in number. *Rom.* iii. 25, "Christ Jesus, whom God has set forth to be a propitiation . . . to declare His righteousness for the remission of sins." Jesus is set forth both as a propitiation and a declaration. Whatever the propitiation means it is made by God. The word used is ἱλαστήριον, and it is the same word which is used in the Septuagint for the covering of the Ark of the Covenant which was sprinkled with the blood of sacrifice, by token that the life of the people was to be a sacrifice to their God. In the same way Christ is regarded as the objective token that (1) The life of God is freely outpoured for the redemption and renewal of men; and (2) The life of man is to be freely offered in sacrifice to God. This is Paul's solitary mention of the word "propitiation." His use is confirmed by John, who, in 1 *Epistle* iv. 10, says, " Herein is love, not that we loved God, but that He loved us, and sent His Son to be a propitiation for our sins"; and again, in ii. 10, he repeats the phrase. Christ is sent of God to propitiate —not Himself surely, who needeth not to be propitiated, but those that are afar off, alienated from the covenant of promise.

2. The second leading word is Reconciliation: where again there is no manner of doubt as to

the plain, strong teaching of the New Testament. I should take as a leading passage the second chapter of the Epistle to the Ephesians. Christ's mission is described there "that He might reconcile both (Jews and Gentiles) unto God in one body by the Cross." The point is that they need to be reconciled to God, not God to them. We have the idea of a loving God entering into our life to break down the wall of partition and win man to Himself and His obedience. Every use of the word is of precisely similar import. I give them briefly. The guiding passage in reference to the Atonement is 2 *Cor.* v. 18 and 19, "All things are of God, *who hath reconciled us to Himself by Jesus Christ*, and hath given to us the ministry of reconciliation, to wit, that God was in Christ reconciling the world unto Himself. . . We pray you in Christ's stead, be ye reconciled to God." The word also occurs in *Heb.* ii. 17, "That He might be a merciful and faithful High Priest in things pertaining to God, to make reconciliation for the sins of the people." The teaching is incontrovertible. The offering and sacrifice are on God's side to produce the necessary effect on the heart of man, end the old estrangement, and make man one with God.

3. The third leading word is Redemption, or ransom. Probably the passages in which the word is used were suggested by Christ's own saying, "The Son of Man is come to give His life a ransom for many." I have always felt that our Lord may have had in His thoughts the great words of *Hosea* (xiii. 14), where the Lord God speaking for Israel says, "I will ransom them from the power of the grave; I will redeem them from death." For indeed it is an Old Testament idea, this of the ransomed of the Lord. Neither can we wonder when we remember how many times the Hebrews were subject to slavery and captivity, and what sacred and inspiring thoughts were associated with the idea of ransom. Yet this is the idea which has been responsible for the most revolting theory of atonement—namely, that Christ was the price paid by God to the devil, in return for which the devil released the enslaved soul from captivity. Now let us look at

what is said. Christ gives His life a ransom ($\lambda \nu \tau \rho \grave{o} \nu$) for the many; these become, in Isaiah's phrase, the ransomed of the Lord. The idea is constant through the Old Testament, where God is pre-eminently the Redeemer of His people. There are scores of passages in this sense, the originality of the Jewish idea lying in redemption without money and without price. This is the idea that Peter introduces into Christian theology, "Ye were not redeemed with corruptible things as silver or gold; but with the precious blood of Christ." This thought of Christ as our Redeemer is set forth in five or six passages all bearing the same sense. There is one passage that contains a somewhat different idea. In *Gal.* iii. 13 we read, "Christ redeemed us from the curse of the law"; indicating deliverance from the bondage of the law and the letter to the freedom of the spirit. Connected with this, too, are such passages as 1 *Cor.* vi. 20, vii. 23, "Ye are bought with a price." Now what is the plain meaning of such teaching as to the redemptive work of Christ? When we read in the *Psalms,* "Who redeemeth thy life from destruction," we understand that God by His love, patience, mercy, saves our life from destruction, and thereby establishes a claim upon it, buying it, redeeming it, for Himself. But suppose you begin to press the argument logically. God keeps my life from destruction; if a life is bought, there must be a purchaser and some one from whom it is purchased. From whom is my life purchased? As to the Redeemer, there is no question; He is the Lord God. As to the captive, there is no question; he is man. But as to the power that holds the soul of man in actual bond there is much question. The old theology said: It is the devil. God must pay the devil his price; the devil's price was Christ; Christ was paid, and the soul of man redeemed thereby. It sounded so logical that men forgot it was so immoral. The idea of the New Testament is not legal and logical. In its simplest form it is this: Thy soul is being destroyed by thy sins; its freedom is lost, and its power with its freedom; the curse of slavery, the slavery of sin and the law, is upon it. Jesus Christ has come to redeem you; but how? By breaking these bonds; by saving you from your sins; by becoming to you the power of God unto salvation. And since this could only be through His sacrifice, emptying Himself, taking upon Him the form of a servant and becoming obedient unto the death of the Cross, that was the price He paid that you might be reached, found, moved, raised from the dead, enfranchised from the bondage of sin and the law. You are hereby bought with a price, even the precious blood of Christ. That is not unthinkable nor incredible.

4. The fourth order of words consists of those translated by our preposition "for." There are two Greek prepositions translated "for": ὑπερ, which means "on behalf of"; and ἀντι, which means "instead of."

(a) ὑπερ is one of the commonest words in the New Testament. Its meaning may be gathered from such a passage as "Pray *for* those who despitefully use you," where, clearly, you are to pray on their behalf. It cannot possibly mean "instead of." Now look at the passages in which this word is used which refer to the Atonement. *Rom.* v. 6: "Christ died *for* the ungodly," *i.e.*, on their behalf; v. 8: "While we were yet sinners Christ died *for* us"—on behalf of us. *Rom.* xiv. 15: "Destroy not with thy meat those *for* whom Christ died." 1 *Peter* iii. 18: "Christ once suffered for sins, the Just *for* the unjust, that he might bring us to God." This should be read in connection with the previous verse, where we are admonished to suffer *on behalf of* righteousness, because Jesus once suffered the Just on behalf of the unjust. Take as a last passage, 2 *Cor.* v. 14: "The love of Christ constraineth us, because we thus judge that One died *for* all, therefore all died." It seems easy to interpret this that One died *instead of* all, so all are counted to have died. But an easy interpretation is often dangerous. Paul's teaching is that Christ's love has such a wonderful power over us that as the result we begin to live, not to ourselves, but just as He lived, absolutely for others. The love of Christ makes us so absolutely one with Him that when He dies *for* all, to benefit and save all, we all die with Him unto self and unto sin.

(b) But now there is the word ἀντι which has but one meaning, "instead of." This meaning you can clearly see in such a saying as the giving of a serpent *for* (instead of) a fish. It is the substitution of one thing for another. It is quite a common word in the New Testament; but there is immense significance in the fact that, with one possible exception, it is never used in passages connected with the doctrine of Atonement. The word meaning "on behalf of" is used; the word meaning "instead of" is not.

The one possible exception is a text quoted already: "The Son of man is come to give His life a ransom *for* many." The word translated "for" in Matthew and Mark is the word ἀντι. The figure of speech here is, of course, taken from the ransom of slaves from their bondage. And it enables us to see what is the truth that lies hidden in all theories of substitution and vicarious suffering. Let us take a simple human illustration. John Smith died in Demerara for the slaves. He died on their behalf; but more, he died instead of them. If they were redeemed from the curse and misery and death of slavery, it was because John Smith died, suffering in their stead. Just in the same way the freedmen of America to-day know that if they are not still enduring the curse of that living death of slavery, it is because John Brown and all his heroic followers died in their stead. These men endured voluntarily death and shame; and because they died other people lived. We read our way into the meaning of Christ's death by such lesser deaths as these. If we are not still in our sins, if we know anything of deliverance from the curse and the death of our trespasses, it is because He died, giving His life a ransom for us.

In conclusion, two great truths stand out: 1. God will save at all costs to the man who is to be saved. 2. God will save at all costs to the Saviour.

As to (1) we see that it is a huge mistake to suppose that the consequence to us of Christ's death is that God lets us off the just punishment of our sins. Where are we told that? We are told the exact opposite; *Heb.* ii. 2: "*Every* transgression and disobedience received the just recompense of reward." No man can sin and not suffer.

But as to (2) we have to face the fact that even the indignation of God against sin, manifested in its immediate and inevitable punishment, does not alone suffice to save. One has often said of some rake of a son, If he could only look into his mother's heart, and see it bleeding and broken; if he could see his sin in the one who loves him most and best, how his sin has been her crucifixion, then he would be overwhelmed in penitence and shame and led to reformation. If the world could look into its Father's heart, and see its sins borne by Him, then it would begin to hate sin and come broken-hearted to His love. This is surely the power of the Cross. With His stripes we are healed. The story of the Gospel is this—God will save at all costs to the Saviour. We see Christ upon the cross, and we realise what our sins contribute to the eternal passion. We learn thus that righteousness is something which is worth all this incalculable cost of sorrow and suffering, pain and discipline. It is not mere hate and horror of sin that we learn from the disclosure of the heart of God in Christ; it is love of righteousness and holiness. We are not made at one with God until we are possessed by this sacred fire of holy love. This is the consummation of Atonement, God in Christ reconciling the world unto Himself.

XV.

BY JOHN HUNTER, D.D.,
Glasgow.

"That they all may be one; as Thou, Father, art in Me and I in Thee, that they also may be one in us. The glory which Thou gavest Me I have given them."—JOHN XVII. 21, 22.

"What we call Christianity is a vast ocean, into which flow a number of spiritual currents of distant and various origin. What is specific in it is Jesus—the religious consciousness of Jesus."—FREDERIC H. AMIEL.

It is ever of supreme and vital moment to bring our religious ideas into harmony with the truth and nature of things. The doctrine of the Atonement, although it is of the essence of Christianity, has undergone constant and radical modification from age to age. It has only to be traced through its successive phases to see a progressive moral evolution. The evolution is not yet finished. Popular representations of it, if they no longer shock our notions of justice and have a demoralising influence, make man's relations to God too strained and artificial. Its generally accepted form belongs to a stage of ethical and religious culture that is passing away, and will have no place in the purer and more spiritual religion of the future.

The profound idea of Reconciliation, which is the heart of the doctrine, has been obscured by interpretations and theories that have allowed too little for the temporal and local conditions under which the apostles lived and thought; and by language which has come through a Christian medium, but not from a Christian source, and in changing its skies has also changed its significance—language which is not the natural and just expression of our spiritual experience, and not in accord with our mental and moral habit. It gets more and more difficult for an increasing number of serious-minded people to find in the mode of representation and style of illustration, which were acceptable to persons passing out of Judaism and Paganism into Christianity, the prototypes and adequate symbols of their Christian faith at the close of the nineteenth century of the era of Christ. They are "faded metaphors" which no longer answer to their sense of truth.

> Not all the blood of beasts
> On Jewish altars slain

can commend the Atonement to their reason or imagination. The ancient symbolism has its place in the history of the Christian teaching, but it is now more calculated to mislead and to confuse than to suggest the real truth. The new wine is bursting the old bottles. The great and final ideas of Christianity are escaping from their long burden of tradition and dogma, and from the Jewish forms which they originally bore, into new and more universal forms. Let those, who honestly can, continue to use the archaic and Hebraistic language of the early teachers of our religion; but playing with words in the exposition of serious and lofty themes often comes dangerously near to grieving the Spirit of Truth. Dante speaks of being obliged to give the words he used a significance which they never had before, but a like exercise of imaginative genius is a somewhat perilous experiment when made by the teacher who to-day seeks to interpret religion. To keep phrases hallowed by tradition and the associations of worship, and then to explain them away by terms which make them mean something entirely different, is a practice that is breeding a profound and fatal distrust of the modern pulpit. Casuistry, obscurantism, and pretending to believe what is not actually believed, ought to find no favour among the disciples of Him who said, "He that is of the truth heareth My voice." We ought to love truth more than we fear departure from tradition, and not be too slow and afraid to separate the Christian ideas from their incidents, accidents, and imperfect products. God hath made us ministers of the New Testament, not of the letter but of the spirit. The present has its claims as well as the past. Religion, like everything else, is subject to the laws of development, and the canon of its Holy Scriptures is never closed. God is eternal and unchangeable, but the revelation of His character and will is continuous and progressive, and man is the child of growth. In the interpretation of the relation of God to His creation and His children, immense progress has been made. To our thought the physical and spiritual universe have both been reconstructed. We are approaching the view of God as a Being essentially united with the universe, the immanent life of all things while transcending all things, requiring no device to bring Him back to a harmony from which He has never departed, revealing Himself in the order of the world, and not by occasional interruptions or breaks in that order. The conception of natural law—law as a principle and method of vital action—has taken the place of juridical law into which past ages ran the idea of redemption. The Church has also grown in grace and the knowledge of its Lord and Saviour. It has rediscovered the secret of Jesus—the large and mighty trust in God as eternal and invincible Goodness, which Jesus quickened in the consciousness of mankind. The reaffirmation of the universal Fatherhood of God in modern days has led to a renaissance of faith, and to a reinterpretation of the entire theology of Christendom. We see God in Christ, and know God by Christ, as never before, and this Divine knowledge is making all things new. The whole range of human life and thought has risen to a higher moral and spiritual level. The doctrine of the Atonement must share in this uplifting and transfiguration of thought and faith and life. It must be put in a way that meets and satisfies our spiritual and intellectual needs, and while doing no violence to what else we know of the world and life, correspond to the truth of Christianity, at least in its simplest expression in the personal message of Jesus Christ. In the past it has been narrowed down to mean one particular thing, and been identified too exclusively with one great historical transaction or event. It is passing out of this limited significance into a larger meaning which holds all that is true in ancient doctrine and infinitely more.

I.—THE NATURE AND NEED OF ATONEMENT.

When we go behind its technical sense we find in the word itself a suggestion of the true and final form of the idea of the Atonement. To be one with God is the Atonement which is the profound and vital need of humanity, and the making of humanity one with God—the process of realising the Divine ideal—is the work of Atonement. Not to be at one with God is for man to be at war with himself, and in imperfect and wrong relations with all other beings and things. Only in moral oneness with God can he find his full and final perfection and peace.

Atonement thus considered is the supreme idea and ultimate purpose of all real religion. In the highest form which religion has reached historically, it receives, both in word and life, its perfect expression. In the prayer of Jesus, "That they all may be one, even as Thou Father art in Me, and I in Thee, that they also may be one in us," the idea of Atonement finds its most spiritual utterance. In the life of Jesus, we see, as in a visible parable, what it is for man to be one with God. He is the historical representative of that perfect union of the human and Divine of which the constitution and experience of man have always been the prophecy.

The essential unity of God and man is the only foundation on which any adequate conception of the Atonement can rest. It is the truth of truths concerning this subject. But the tendency of religion in its cruder forms has ever been to emphasize and magnify the distance between God and man, and out of the attempt to reduce that separation have come the gross ideas of sacrifice which, passing over into Christian thought, have gathered about the Cross and put it to an open shame. We must learn to think of God as in man and his life, and not as outward, separate and remote, coming near only by arbitrary miracle and related only by artificial conjunction. The idea of union with God is involved in the idea of man. The genealogy of man as man has no zoological root. His childhood to God is the most radical fact of his being. He is God's offspring, begotten, not made. Deity and humanity are not two alien natures, but one nature. The essential life of man is akin to the essential life of God. Reason, thought, feeling, justice, truth, mercy, and love are kindred in God and man. The Divine is but the human seen in its source and perfection. "I and My Father are one" is in idea true of all humanity.

God and man are in idea one; but the fulfilment of that ideal is the long and slow work of God and man "labouring together" in the succession of ages. Not in any first man do we see the ideal relation between God and man realised. The sublime affirmation of the Hebrew seer, "God made man in His own image," is prophecy, not history—the end seen from the beginning. It is the last and not the first Adam that bears the image of the heavenly. The manifestation of the sons of men as the sons of God is not the starting-point, but the goal of human progress. History is the story of the making of man in the Divine image; it reveals man becoming less animal and more spiritual, climbing up from low estate to the true life of a son of God—to sit with Christ on His throne. In Jesus Christ we see the Messiah of the spiritual evolution, the mark of

our high calling, showing us what we realise
slowly, the type and promise of our ultimate
perfection and destiny.

What the Atonement means is a matter to be
determined by the facts of our nature and condition. It is clearly not a lost unity that has to
be restored. Man cannot have departed from
a type which he has never realised, fallen away
from a standard he has never reached. Union
with God is a moral relation to be attained,
not preserved. The race of mankind has never
been more one with God than it is to-day.

> In Adam's fall
> We sinned all

is theory, not fact. The Christian doctrine of
Atonement is not bound up with any such un-
scientific and unhistorical positions. It is the
rise, not the fall, of man with which the study
of history makes us acquainted. The advance,
it is true, has been painfully slow and gradual,
and not without reversions; but looking largely
at history,

> Since time began
> We see the steady gain of man.

There is a Divine order which no disorders can disturb, and to which falls are but stages of evolution. We are living in a growing, not in a blasted world, under God's love and blessing, not under God's wrath and curse. Imperfection is no proof of depravity. Tendencies must be distinguished from results, and powers and passions, good in their right degree, be separated in thought from their misdirection and perversion. It is from an outworn view of human nature there has come the idea that the natural development of man must inevitably be that of constant and chronic enmity against goodness and God. Growth is the law of the world. The sense of sin is not the sign of degeneration, but of a moral uprising. It is, as Carlyle says, "the beginning of all progress," and until it is awakened, man is little more than an animal. What we see, when we look back, is man rising through many struggles to his true life, seeking God by a law of his being. "Nearer, my God, to Thee," "Restless, till I rest in Thee," are words which interpret the conscious and unconscious aspiration and movement of man's whole life upon this earth. Because man is what he is he cannot remain satisfied in the outer circles of being, or endure to be far away from Him who is the Beginning and the End of his life. Toward and into that inner circle of unity between Father and Son he must press and enter, if his life is to be anything but a living death. From this point of view, the Atonement that is a vital human need, is no making up of a previous strife, but the fulfilment of the Divine idea of man. It is effected through self-development and self-realisation. Man comes to God as he comes to himself; and to come to himself he must come to God.

Atonement is, further, the reconciliation of the whole man, and his whole life and world, to God. To be one with God is to be one with the entire truth and order of things with which man and God, working together, have to do. The physical, intellectual, moral and spiritual life of man, his personal and social life in all their relations and aspects, are one life in the Divine idea, and have to be brought into conformity with the Divine purpose and will. A high and noble reconciliation is possible between the lower and higher elements of human nature, and on it depend our inward peace and outward power and progress. Good and evil within us are not separate powers and passions, but degrees of the same thing, the right use good, the abuse only evil. The union of the mind of man with the Absolute Mind, the correspondence of his thought with fact and truth, is the aspect which the Atonement takes in the region of the intellectual life. Thinking as we please, believing as we like, is the alienation of the mind from God. It is the teaching of all experience that we are conditioned morally, as well as physically, and can only develop healthily as we follow certain lines which, though implicated in our nature and revealed in our experience, are no more the creation of experience than are the laws which keep and guide the stars in their courses. The Divine order for men in social relations is clearly meant to be that of a family; and we are only in our right, or righteous, state when we are living and working together fraternally.

We cannot be one with God until we are one with our fellows, cannot be within the circle of right universal relations until we are in right relations with those who are nearest to us. The self-regardful type of life is enmity against God. Reconciliation to the laws of justice, love and brotherhood is reconciliation to God. The laws which regulate the immediate communion of the soul with God are more subtle and less capable of exact expression than those which regulate our physical and social life; yet there is a Divine order here without variableness, an order which is revealed and confirmed by all religious experience. It is the pure in heart who see God; it is he who dwelleth in love who dwelleth in God; and it is what St. John calls "the Son," the filial mind and spirit in man, that brings him to the Father.

Reconciliation to our earthly lot, with all its fixed and inevitable conditions and issues, is another aspect of the Christian idea of Atonement. To be at peace with God is to be at peace with things, with all the things which God has ordained for our human discipline; at peace with the laws of labour and struggle and change, with the laws of life and death. And it is just in proportion as man brings himself, or is brought, into conformity and harmony with the laws that control and guide his destiny, and with the whole idea and order of his being and life, that union with God becomes a reality, reconciliation is effected and the Atonement practically completed. There is no other way of Atonement than the way of obedience—every man's free obedience to the Divine laws of his being and life.

But who is thus at one with God? It is the selfish will and order, not the Divine will and order, which is more or less universally followed and obeyed. Man everywhere is in conflict with himself because he is in conflict with the Divine will, because he is at strife with the order which God has ordained for him and his life, because his powers and affections are estranged from God and are restless in their departure from Him. It is only by a figure of speech we can speak of breaking

God's laws. We fail to obey them, set ourselves against them, and they break us. The moral order requires no special and external vindication of its majesty. God does not need to be appeased, for His laws never fail to punish sin in their own good time and way. But compensation He does not exact or need. It is not the suffering of the sinner, but his restoration to goodness and a life of conscious harmony with the Divine will that satisfies the holy and righteous God. Propitiation, expiation, and substitution, in their current interpretations and forms, are as little in accord with what we see to be the order of things in the universe as they are with the tone and tendency of the teaching of Jesus and the real and profound needs of the enlightened soul.

II.—THE WORK OF GOD IN THE WORLD IS THE WORK OF ATONEMENT.

Creatorhood and Fatherhood have their obligations and duties as well as creaturehood and childhood. The Creator cannot leave His creation unfinished. The Father must seek to be one with His children and to bring them to perfection. We had no choice of existence, but He from whom we came, if only to satisfy Himself, will have regard to the work of His hands and respond to the appeal, "I am Thine, save me." The movement will not be all, or chiefly, on the side of man. It is the essential nature of love to seek and to save. The righteousness and blessedness of man are necessary to God.

The work of Atonement is God's eternal work. We cannot conceive of the Divine Goodness as ever being insensate and passive, or as other than ceaselessly compassionate and helpful. The life of sacrifice is the law of love for heaven as for earth. Because God is love, to create is to suffer, and to call mankind into being is to be afflicted in its afflictions. Wholly outside His world God has never been; He has been always in it, bearing the sins and carrying the sorrows of our race. It was not a new and strange work the Beloved Son of God came to do, but the work which He saw His Father doing continuously. The Divine mission of

Jesus is not so much an isolated interpolation in human history as the reflection and revelation of the universal and eternal labour, passion and sacrifice of God. Without Jesus the world was for thousands of years, but not without the merciful, gracious, and redeeming God. "His goings forth have been of old and from everlasting." The whole economy of things is so ordered as to bring men at every point into contact with God. This is the final meaning and end of all the forces that enter into human life. By all the natural processes and experiences of life, by the discipline of hardship and toil, joy and sorrow, by the retribution that warns us back to right, and the moral purpose that is in all events, God from the beginning has been reducing and destroying the separation between Himself and His children.

But the work of God on man is not so much a forcing process from without as an inducing process from within. Influence, not coercion, is the Divine method. Immanent in all men, He co-operates with the aspiration and effort of every man toward light and goodness, and therefore with the universal movement of the race. He is the ultimate Cause of progress and the Unseen Source and inspiration of all our human strivings to draw near unto Him—even of those very strivings which in our ignorance we make with a view to reconcile Him. We seek Him because He first seeks us. The spirit of truth and goodness is His Spirit, and what we find of that spirit in ourselves and in others, in this age and in all ages, proves that God is ever nigh to our humanity, giving an atoning energy and effect to all noble striving and sacrifice.

The Divine action on man is mediate as well as immediate—through men, whom God raises up, endows and inspires, and in whom He lives and suffers, and by whom He makes known His character and will, and reconciles the world unto Himself. Many have taken part in this Divine ministry of reconciliation before, as after, the Advent of the Son of God. Revelation is especially the means of Atonement, revelation that has grown clearer from age to age, as men have become more developed morally and more sensitive and receptive spiritually. God must be known for men to become one with Him. A true knowledge of God removes the fear that is born of ignorance, and quickens in human souls that spirit of faith which is the strength and salvation of humanity.

III.—The Work of Atonement Specialised in Jesus Christ.

The most remarkable and characteristic thing about Jesus, and that which gives the keynote to His place and mission in the world, is His absolute renouncement of the idea that He said or did anything of Himself. "Not I, but my Father," is the sum and substance of His teaching concerning Himself. It is the Father's work into which the Son enters. It is not Christ apart from God, but God in Christ, said the apostle, who is reconciling the world to Himself.

The entire manifestation of the Son of God, and not merely the death on the cross, was and is the power of Atonement in the life of Jesus

Christ. With Him there entered a new and Divine power into human history. Those who are unable to separate the Incarnation from the normal processes of human life, nevertheless see in it the climax and crown of a vast upward movement which in all its great stages was a Divine revelation. Whatever prophecies there may have been of the Divine Sonship of humanity in the experience of men in the past, it came forth into clear and complete consciousness for the first time in Him who said, " I and My Father are one." It is this perfect realisation of filial union and communion with God that is the central fact of our Christian faith. The consciousness of Sonship to God is also the distinctively Christian experience. By all the methods of personal influence Christ quickens in human souls prepared to receive it His own sense of filial relationship to the Father of spirits. Drawn by sympathy into spiritual intimacy with Him, they are drawn by Him into filial intimacy with His Father. "As many as received Him to them gave He power to become sons of God." Further, it is the filial spirit that Christ quickens in human hearts that is the medium of our communion with God, and, when fully attained, it makes God and man at one and at peace. It is this experience of sonship produced and perfected in man, and not an external historical transaction, that is pre-eminently and peculiarly the atoning work of Jesus Christ. (It is in the Gospel of St. John we find the Atonement presented as a fact of consciousness or experience. The Johannean Atonement has been set over against the Pauline Atonement, but the contradiction is not so inward and radical as it is often represented to be. When St. Paul gets clear of Judaistic, and other entanglements, and rises into the pure air of absolute truth, his word is not essentially different from that of the apostle of spiritual religion.)

The whole ministry of Christ, from its beginning to its close, was a ministry of reconciliation—a power of Atonement. By what He was, what He said, and what He did, He sought to make God known, to save men from those false ideas of the Divine character and ways which set human thought and feeling wrong, to expel suspicion and fear from their hearts, and to make them realise that they were His Father's children, and had no right therefore to despise themselves or despair of themselves. They saw in His compassion the Divine compassion, in His love the revelation and assurance of the Divine love, in His forgiveness the type and promise of the Divine forgiveness. Coming to know God as He is revealed in Jesus Christ is to trust and rejoice in God and to have sympathies and harmonies created where previously dwelt antipathies and antagonisms. When on earth our Lord also sought to make men in all the relations and provinces of their life at one with the Divine Will. He fought against disease, ignorance, injustice, hate and all forms of selfishness as the enemies of God and man. The great burden of His message was God's Kingdom, God's order, and He suffered and died daily to reconcile men to the Divine order of their life.

The Cross, although it embodied no principle that was not illustrated in His life, was yet the crowning manifestation of the principle, of the law, purpose, and spirit of His life. It was the sign and symbol of the perfect identification of Himself with man and with God. It was no wonder that in a strain of prophecy He looked forward to the Cross as the means of raising Him above all the mists and clouds of mortal misunderstanding, prejudice, and hatred, to a moral height where He would be seen in all the glory of His Divine obedience and charity, and from which He would draw to Himself the love and loyalty of mankind.

No word sums up and expresses more fully the influence of Jesus Christ than the word Atonement. By what He was and said and did by the power of His spirit and the affections He quickens, He makes men, to-day as yesterday, at one with God, at one with their fellows, at one with themselves, and at one with life in all its larger and deeper meanings and ends. The history of the religion of Jesus is a history of Atonement. That short life, to all appearance, crushed and ended on the Cross, has expanded into the life of Christendom, and been an endless power of progress. The faith and spirit of Christ, wherever they go, subdue discords, heal alienations, harmonise differences, and so make peace.

IV.—The Atonement an Unfinished, Continuous and Progressive Work.

The Atonement was not completed when Jesus finished His work on earth. In Him it found and finds its ideal fulfilment, but not its actual completion. The isolation of His work from the universal work of God in the world and from the work of the Church (that is, the Christian part of humanity) is wholly without warrant in the New Testament. Both in Gospel and Epistle, and with endless richness of appeal, men are called to be what Jesus was and to do what He did. All the great things attributed to Him are expected and demanded of His followers. It is one of the unspeakable results of His influence on men that they are moved to follow in His footsteps, take up His Cross, fill up that which is behind of His sufferings and become active sharers in that

Divine, eternal sacrifice by which the world is being delivered from its evil. It is not by imputing, but imparting righteousness; not by substituting His obedience for ours, but by inspiring us to obey; not by displacing, but reinforcing our personal will and activity, Jesus Christ is the power of God and the wisdom of God. The outward facts of His life, the Crucifixion and Resurrection especially, only gain their real and highest meaning when they are translated into moral and spiritual experiences, and we are able to say with St. Paul, "I am crucified with Christ"; "I am risen with Christ." It is not by any outward reliance on what Jesus was and what He did the world is to be saved, but by men, who, through the power of His Spirit, have been brought into moral union with God, and are inspired by the passion of the Cross, entering into the work of Christ and prolonging and repeating His sacrifice in their own lives. They are the hiding-place of His power, and His ever-renewed and ever-growing body. "As Thou hast sent Me into the world, so have I sent them into the world." "The glory which Thou gavest Me I have given them." Bearing the sorrows and iniquities of the world, taking away its sin by the sacrifice of Himself, helping to reconcile it to God—this is what every man is doing who bears worthily the name of the Crucified, and lives and burns in His fellowship.

Every Sunday in thousands of churches God is thanked for "the redemption of the world by our Lord Jesus Christ." That thanksgiving, when thoughtfully offered, is inspired by faith and hope. For what we see around us is not a world really redeemed, but only a world that is being redeemed. The actual redemption of humanity is coincident with its moral and spiritual progress, and can only be accomplished by the slow and constant operation of the Spirit and Power of God. But the Divine power is no abstraction, and the Divine Spirit no wandering ghost. The unit of power is not God nor man in isolation. God in the world, reconciling it to Himself, means God and man working together, the Divine power and Spirit in human hearts and lives, permeating and quickening them as the infusion of a higher life. The Atonement is still in process of completion. Into the Son's work, which is also the Father's, we are called to enter; called to hasten, by our life and labour, the time of the great Reconciliation, when man's moral being shall be received into the unity of creation, and things in heaven and on earth shall be one, and God, that is Good, be all in all!

> Dear Father of the human heart,
> The whole wide world atone;
> What Thou hast been to us, impart
> To all; make all Thine own.

XVI.

BY FRÉDERIC GODET, D.D.,
Neuchâtel, Switzerland.

I BELIEVE that all the writers who up to now have taken part in the symposium in *The Christian World* on this central question of Christianity are agreed in rejecting the notion of Expiation in the pagan sense; the sense, that is, according to which the man who had offended a divinity must, in order to appease his resentment and recover his favour, pay the equivalent of his trespass either by a sacrifice offered or by some form of suffering undergone. This pagan idea is not that of the Bible. There, not only in the New Testament, but already in the Old, it is God, the offended God Himself, who takes the initiative in His own reconciliation with the sinful world; who determines the conditions of it, and who provides the means for its realisation. "The Lord hath laid on Him (His servant) the iniquity of us all" (*Isa.* liii.). "Blessed is he whose sin is covered and to whom the Lord imputeth not iniquity" (*Psa.* xxxii.). "God so loved the world that He gave His only begotten Son" (*John* iii.). "All things are of God, who hath reconciled us to Himself through Jesus Christ" (2 *Cor.* v.). "Ye have been redeemed by the precious blood of Christ, as of a lamb without blemish. . . fore-ordained from before the foundation of the world" (1 *Pet.* i.). These and similar passages teach that the redemption of the world by Christ is due absolutely to the Divine love.

But this being so, it may seem a misnomer to speak of God's reconciliation with man, since He who decides on, and accomplishes the reconciliation can hardly be regarded as needing to be Himself reconciled. The love that loves sufficiently to take such an action towards the offender is surely in no need of being itself regained. We must then, say some, eliminate entirely from Christianity the notion of expiation and, still more, of substitution, preserving only the idea of the Heavenly Father, ever ready to pardon without any other condition than that of man's faith in His love—a faith by which the sinner finds himself really reconciled with the God whom before he had regarded as his enemy. This is, in appearance, an important simplification of the Christian doctrine, and in support of it, it is usual to cite the parable of the prodigal son.

It has, however, to be observed that the New Testament offers to us in various forms—sometimes as verb, sometimes as substantive—a term which it is difficult to reconcile with this point of view. Five times do we meet there the Greek term which signifies the placating, or rendering favourable, of God. (*Luke* xviii. 13; *Rom.* iii. 24; *Heb.* ii. 17; 1 *John* ii. 2, and iv. 10.) This, while it does not exactly imply the destruction of a feeling of enmity in God, supposes nevertheless a favourable change to be produced in Him towards the sinner. Paul indeed goes so far as to speak of "indignation," of "wrath," which he attributes to God against those who "obey unrighteousness" (*Rom.* ii. 8). He further (in *Eph.* ii. 3) calls all men in their natural condition, "children of wrath." According to this there is room for the idea that the term "reconciliation" may apply not only to man, but also to God. When Paul (*Rom.* xi. 28) calls the Jews "enemies," "as touching the Gospel," and "for your sake," but on the other hand declares them "beloved for the fathers' sake," it is clear that the word "loved" can only relate to the love of God, and that consequently the word "enemies" in this connection means also the (momentary) enmity of God towards these same Jews. So in *Rom.* v. 9, 10, where we find the same word "enemy" used directly after the phrase "the wrath of God," it is impossible to confine the term entirely to the enmity of man towards God. The apostle is evidently thinking at the same time of God's enmity against sinful man. The work of reconciliation, then, while, as all Scripture says, having God as its author, has nevertheless, it appears, a certain bearing upon the Divine mind, and the idea of a propitiation which occurs so often in the New Testament, and applying, as it must, to an effect produced upon God, however difficult it may be to accord with the fact that God is at the same time its author, finds yet its right to a place in the Christian dogma.

To understand how that is possible it is necessary, first of all, to distinguish between the love which *gives* and the love which *pardons*. Both are indeed the same love, but their action is governed by different conditions. The former has nothing to do but to yield itself to its feeling of free benevolence, and to simply scatter its gifts; but the latter, at the moment of action, finds two obstacles in its way. These are, on the one hand, the sentiment of displeasure in the offended party, and on the other, the disastrous and wide-spreading effects which would follow from a pardon pure and simple, and granting, as it would seem, the right of existence to evil. The love which pardons can, then, only be exercised on two conditions that are unknown to the love which gives. The first is the breaking down of the repulsion, the alienation of heart, the revolt which the offence produces in the offended party. And when the offended one is God, to whom the good is not, as with us, a something apart from or above Him, but who is Himself Goodness in Person, what a supreme gravity belongs, then, to the offence! The revolt of man against God becomes nothing less than a negation of God, that is to say, of the good, and God cannot but react against what amounts to a denial of Himself. From the perfect holiness which constitutes His essence there results, therefore, an active indignation which is opposed to pardon. The second obstacle is, as we have said, the danger lest sin, unless it meet with an adequate chastisement as the opposer of good, be not in some way, as it were, legitimised. To pardon it unconditionally would be to yield it an enduring place in the life of humanity.

It is to these two exigences that an expiation, in the Christian sense of the word, must respond. It is true that Paul does not apply the term "reconciliation" to God Himself. He does not say that God has reconciled Himself to the world, but that "God has reconciled the world to Himself through Christ" (2 *Cor.* v. 18, 19). Did he shrink from employing the first expression, as though it might seem to suggest an imputation against the Divine Majesty? However that may be, he himself calls Christ "the means of propitiation set forth by God" (*Rom.* iii. 25), and in 2 *Cor.* v. 20, 21, he justifies the invitation to be reconciled to God which the preachers of the Gospel are to address to men by this motive: "For God has made sin for us Him who knew no sin"; in other words: "Be ye reconciled with God, since God Himself has become reconciled to you; since He has done in relation to His own nature what was necessary for that end."

But does not this idea suppose a change in the Divine mind incompatible with the Divine immutability? We may grant the change. But if we admit that God rejoices over the spectacle of a man devoted to goodness and opposing evil, that His heart goes out to such an one, and that His power co-operates with him; and if, on the other hand, it is certain that the heart of God is grieved, alienated, outraged, at the view of a man obstinately bent on evil, how can it be otherwise than that when a change shall in either of these cases take place towards good or evil, a corresponding change shall be produced in the mind of God? When the man changes, if the Divine sentiment did not also change in relation to him, that would be really to say that God was changeable. Love of good and hatred of evil form the invariable law of His being, and from this it results that each instant infinite changes take place in the mind of God in accordance with the moral condition of His creatures. We must not represent to ourselves the Divine immutability as though it were like that of a stone; it is comparable rather to that of a column of mercury, which, in constant obedience to the same physical law, rises or falls in the tube in perfect accord with each change in the atmosphere. As a friend once said to me, God is, of all beings, the most delicately and infinitely sensitive. From afar He sees and rejoices over the first movement of a heart that turns towards good; and equally does He perceive and is grieved by, the faintest drawing of the soul towards evil.

Precisely because the Divine love is so perfectly free is it able to take on differing forms. Of these I single out two which have a special bearing on our subject. God's love may show itself as a love of compassion or as a love of satisfaction and of complaisance in its object. The love of compassion reveals itself in God as a necessity for consoling, for saving. It is perfectly compatible with hatred of evil, and with indignation against one who commits it. One may say, indeed, that the greater God's indignation, the more profound the compassion He feels for the evil condition of the man who causes it. For man is miserable to the extent in which he displeases God; and that God Himself well knows. Hence His pity. It is from this love of compassion that the design proceeds of saving the sinful world. The love of satisfaction or of complacency, on the contrary, results from the joy which fills the heart of God at seeing the realisation of good in His creature, whom He can now lead into full communion with Himself, a communion which is man's supreme good, the final object of his existence. The transition from the first of these forms of Divine love to the second can, naturally, result only from a transformation in the object of it, and that by an inner movement from an evil to a good will.

What, then, will be the condition under which the perfect love of God, the love of satisfaction and of communion, can replace the love, as yet incomplete, of compassion? This result will necessarily depend on a change in the moral condition of the world itself, in a turning from sin to goodness. But how can this be brought about? To this question, the gravest with which the human spirit can be confronted, the Gospel contains the answer. The whole life of Jesus was a manifestation of holiness and of communion with God, calculated by its exquisite beauty to awaken on the part of all who were its witnesses the aspiration for a similar perfection. But if this homage rendered to the majesty of goodness could exert in human hearts a hunger for holiness, it was not sufficient to repair the outrage offered to the Divine authority by human disobedience.

Against this disobedience, flaunting itself so shamelessly in the world, there was need of a further protest than this simple example of a perfectly holy life; there needed a definite repudiation of this revolt of the creature, one which should constitute a solemn disassociation from it of the human will. This decisive condemnation of sin could alone restore to the Divine holiness the glory which had been obscured and the authority that had been disowned.

This was the work accomplished, first of all, in the inner consciousness of Jesus. As the Jewish high priest who, in the holy of holies, before the Ark, symbol of the Divine throne, confessed the sins of the whole people personified in him; so Jesus, in communion with the human family of which He had, by the fact of His birth, become a member, Jesus, the only righteous, the only One whose conscience was at the height of the Divine holiness, in the deepest depth of His being, condemned human sin, as God condemned it. By an unfathomable prodigy of love He entered into the horror of the sins of which He was each day witness, as though He had Himself been the responsible author of them; and in the perfect union of His conscience with the Divine holiness, in this *rencontre intime* between God and Himself, He pronounced the condemnation to death of human sin, a sentence destined to be ratified later by the united conscience of all humanity.

Sin, then, has been judged by man in this one typical, normal conscience, as God Himself judges it in Heaven; not this or that sin, but sin in itself, which Jesus bore before God as though He had been the sole sinner upon earth. There took place there, in the conscience of Christ, between the Divine holiness and human sin, an encounter the mystery of which St. Peter compares to an abyss of which the angels themselves cannot sound the depths, but of which we may get some idea in listening to that cry of Jesus, "My God, My God, why hast Thou forsaken Me?" The abandonment to which God delivers over the sinner had at that moment become His portion. This is what Paul describes in other terms when he says:

"God hath made Him to be sin for us." This cry of anguish, of immense sorrow, which broke from the heart of Jesus into the ear of God, brought appeasement; for that is the exact sense of the word which the Scripture uses to designate what took place in the heart of God. Here was the reparation, the true expiation in the Christian sense of the word. It is the act by which the offender himself condemns his sin, and by that condemnation, so far as depends on himself, makes it to utterly disappear.

It is true that it was in one conscience alone that this judgment of the world's sin, the echo of that which God pronounces in heaven, took place. But as there is only one rationality in all intelligent minds, so in reality there is only one and the same conscience in all moral beings; and thus it is that the cry of suffering which came from that one perfectly normal conscience is yet to re-echo in all other human consciences. There was in this solemn meeting between the Most Holy and the typal representative of humanity the dawn, as it were, of a new world yet to appear and to replace that condition of revolt which has reigned from the time of the Fall. Just as a change in the mode of existence and of action of the magnetic pole would be enough to bring about a movement and a transformation in the magnetic state of the whole world, so this transformation in the relation of man to God of which the heart of Christ was at once the operator and the theatre, in restoring God and man to their true place, has sufficed to bring into immediate prospect a similar revolution in the human conscience, and, it may be, everywhere where beings exist possessed of this Divine organ.

And it is this mighty and sacred reaction, the signal for which was given by the conscience of the Head of humanity, that, with its happy consequences, foreseen and willed, has formed the decisive fact whose action has so wrought upon God, transforming His love of compassion, as author of redemption, into a yet nobler love, that of satisfaction, of a communion with humanity full of tenderness, whence results the communication of His Spirit.

At the same time this reparation accomplished in the conscience of Jesus could not remain as a simple interior fact, known only to God; it must be made manifest externally, in order that its action might extend over the entire human family. The Moral Substitution which we have just been describing needed undoubtedly to come first; for it is the very soul of, and gives its whole value to, the external reparation. But the death of the Cross required to be added to it, in order to reveal to all eyes the serious reality of the moral work, and that it might become the object of faith. It is a law derived from the Divine holiness, that suffering, interior or exterior, is the inevitable consequence of sin. This law is the safeguard of the sinner himself, since it is by penalty alone that he is made to feel the necessity of repentance. Jesus accepted the application of this law to Himself under the most rigorous of forms. But the element of reparation in the death of the Cross did not consist in the unspeakable sufferings which accompanied it. That lay in the silent and absolute submission with which they were endured. It is not a suffering merely undergone which reconciles; it is a suffering accepted, recognised as just. The child who revolts against its punishment has offered no reparation at all. The Cross, accepted by Jesus without resistance or murmur, was the striking manifestation of that interior judgment which He had just pronounced before God upon the sin of humanity. St. Paul said (*Galatians* iii. 13) that Jesus was made a curse for us, and this by having hung upon the cross, according to the saying, "Cursed is he who hangeth on the tree." This exterior substitution is at once the consequence and the complement of the moral substitution described above.

It is on this double substitution—the moral and the exterior—that the Christian Atonement rests. And now—it is our last question—What is needed that each separate human being shall participate in the "Divine appeasement" of which the Scriptures speak, and in that return to grace which is the consequence? One thing. He who aspires to salvation must associate himself by faith in that travail of soul accomplished in the heart of Christ when He consented to be "made sin for us"; he must look upon his sin with the same sense of reprobation; unite himself with the sorrowing confession of Jesus, with His humble appeal to the Divine mercy when, before His Father, He judged sin as God judges it, and pronounced its sentence of death as God Himself pronounces it. This personal association with the sacred act of which the soul of Jesus had been the theatre was mysteriously wrought in the heart of that savage Bechuana who, on hearing the story of the Cross, deeply moved, exclaimed, "Jesus away from there! That is my place!"

Jesus Himself used an image which contains indeed the same thought when He says, "I am come to serve, and to give My life a ransom for many." A ransom is paid for the captive whom it is desired to liberate, for the criminal we would deliver from punishment. That is the service Jesus came to render to humanity, once slave and criminal, the slave of sin and worthy of condemnation. To accomplish this double redemption He did not offer the sacrifice of some personal good that He might have enjoyed; He offered up His own life, His very person, body and soul; He, the innocent One, consenting to be made responsible before God for the sin of the world, and to be treated as such before the eyes of world. If I may so say, He descended into the gloomy prison-house where we lay, and in entering left open the door behind Him, that each captive who recognised in Him his ransom might secure his release and enjoy once more the pure outside air; that each—to drop the figure—might seize with the hand of faith, the greatest of all life's goods, peace with God, and the re-establishment of communion with Him.

The work of deliverance which Jesus wrought by the offering up of Himself did not end with the death of the Cross. As the Risen and Glorified One He continues it in the heavenly life by His work of intercession before God, as says St. Paul (*Rom.* viii. 34) and John (1 *John* ii. 1), and as is vividly set forth in the Epistle to the Hebrews (*Heb.* vii. 25), "Who ever liveth to make intercession for us." The work of expiation accomplished here below was the point of departure for this heavenly intercession which is its simple continuation.

Every time that, by faith's assimilation, the "for us" becomes a "for me," at once a sorrowful and joyous "for me," in the heart of man, and that to this "He for me" there comes as answer in the heart a grateful "I for Him," that heart is henceforth not only the object of God's compassionate love, but also of that love of His which is satisfied, which adopts, which communes. The guilty child is folded in the arms of the Father. He has found grace. He was dead and is alive again.

I suppose that *The Christian World*, in seeking the views of so large a number of Christian writers on this supreme topic, has not so much wished for profound dissertations as for a personal profession of faith, with more or

less of the grounds of it. Well, this is mine.
The " For me," understood as in the sense of
" in my place," is, in my eyes, the centre of the
Gospel, as it is the nerve of the Christian life.
Christianity deprived of this becomes nothing
more than a sword with its edge blunted,
powerless in the hands both of the missionary
who seeks to strike down other religions, and in
that of the private Christian to deal a mortal
blow at the heart of the old man, at the
tyrannous domination of self. The Christ
who became my substitute on the Cross has
alone the right and the power to be substitute
in my heart. "For the love of Christ constraineth us, because we thus judge that if one
died for all, therefore all died; and He died for
all that they which live should no longer live
unto themselves, but unto Him who for their
sakes died and rose again." So says Paul
(2 *Cor.* v. 14, 15).

Jesus, praying in Gethsemane, at the moment
when He penetrated to the depths of our dark
prison, cried "Father, with Thee all things are
possible"; as though He Himself no longer

saw clearly the necessity, in order to the world's salvation, of all that was awaiting Him. Nevertheless, He submitted. And for ourselves, who are still, in part, in the twilight, is not this light, though imperfect, yet enough for our belief and obedience?

If in these lines I have in any degree missed the truth, may God pardon me. During the sixty years that I have meditated this question I have found nothing better. "She hath done what she could."

XVII.

BY T. T. MUNGER, D.D.

IF an intelligent man, having laid aside all preconceptions of the Atonement, were to begin the study of it afresh, the first thing he would notice is that it has not only passed through many phases, but that mutually excluding theories of it have been held, and that these theories bear each the impress of its age and often of its region, and reflect the environing social institutions. Having made this discovery, he begins to suspect all the theories, and is ready either for utter denial, or to say that there must be a reality behind each which the theory beclouds and perverts.

As he continues his study he finds that each theory is sub-divided by minor or qualifying theories, and that these often bear the impress of some individual mind or some school of philosophy. His distrust returns, and with dismay he asks, Is it possible that the truth on which hangs the salvation of the world is a matter to be defined, first by one set of men, and then by another, and finally by one man? Is it fixed by some age, or some civilisation, or some strong intellect with a peculiar experience or temperament? Worst of all, is it shaped so as to fit in with other doctrines, *e.g.*, limited in its extent because required by a doctrine of decrees?

At this point he is again tempted to throw up the subject in disgust at the way in which it has been handled, and leave it buried under the contradictions and absurdities heaped upon it. But he again restrains himself, reflecting that only some great reality could provoke such diversity of thought and outlive so rough usage. He will not infer that each theory contains some truth of its own, nor will he say that it is a great mystery, and is capable of showing many sides, with others yet to be revealed. Tell that to any man of real thought, he says, and straightway you make an infidel of him. It is one of those pious sophistries by which men seek to add to the glory of God, in disregard of Luther's warning " to abstain from the curious teaching of God's majesty." The world is not saved by a mystery, but by a revelation. In some sense, indeed, truth grows ever brighter, but to involve it in one's own ignorance and call it a mystery is not to glorify God, nor to define truth. More and more does our seeker become convinced that the theories simply neutralise one another, and that, so far as throwing any light upon the truth itself is concerned, they may be left by the wayside as milestones to mark their distance from the generic fact out of which they sprang. For that he begins to search, and he finds it, of course, in Christ Himself. One thing he has gained, and an immense gain it is, he has got rid of theory and dogma, and come into the presence of a *Life*.

The Atonement as a dogma, in all its various theories, rests upon a basis of other dogmas that are fast disappearing. Indeed, these fading dogmas created the various theories. The fall in Adam, federal headship, the consequent total apostasy and guilt of all mankind, the curse of God pronounced upon all, election to salvation or destruction—these dogmas demanded and shaped the Atonement according to the way in which they were interpreted. A thorough-going doctrine of election and reprobation created a limited Atonement. As its rigidity yielded, the Atonement was declared to be universal. Thus every new phase of the doctrine reflected some new phase of the dogmas. But the dominating factor was not the Atonement, but some dogma of depravity, or Divine sovereignty, or justice, or sacrifice; and as these were always changing, the Atonement was refined in order to secure harmony in the system. Thus, what was first was made last; and what should have shaped and directed all theology became what the prevailing notions chanced to make it. It would be idle to refer to these past phases of the doctrine that go along with Ptolemaism and mediævalism, as of like standing, if they did not linger still, and if there were not a disposition to recur to them, or to something like them. A dogma becomes entrenched in a creed, and the creed is entrenched in an ecclesiasticism, which·again is entrenched in the love and veneration of multitudes of men and women. To dislodge it is both difficult and dangerous, and often it is better to leave it to the eradicating force of growing intelligence and to the upheavals which cannot be repressed. The Presbyterian Church in America is in a chronic state of unrest and threatening disruption because, along with other differences, a part read *Genesis* literally and hold to the expiatory view of the Atonement, while another part read it in the light of modern criticism and incline to the governmental view, or leave the doctrine untouched.

But while waiting may sometimes be a necessity, no opportunity should be lost to carry the doctrine back—past all creeds and churches and systems, even to the ignoring of history, and lay it down where only it belongs, namely, upon the life of Christ Himself. He is the doctrine. It had its beginning, its development and its fulfilment in Him, because as the Son of God He represents the eternal humanity in God the Father. He did not leave the truth, which was the heart of His work, half taught. He finished the work given Him to do. It was complete because He summed up in Himself the life of humanity, from which no teaching essential to its salvation was left out. So much we must say, unless we relegate Christ to the level of a mere Teacher, and put His Church over instead of under Him.

Now, who was Christ; where did He stand; what did He teach; how came He to die, and in what manner, and with what thoughts in His mind?—large questions, to which only briefest answers can here be attempted.

First of all, Christ was in the line of the prophets, and not of the priests. If it be said that He is our Priest as well as Prophet, the priest is to be interpreted by the Prophet. No priest appeared on the Mount of Transfiguration. He asserted that His death was the fulfilment of "the Scriptures of the prophets," not of the priests, though the Old Testament was full of sacrificial ritual. The ancient antagonism did not die out, but lived on in Him because the prophet had superseded the priest;

the life takes the place of the sacrifice; the man himself becomes the altar and the offering. Thus, by the very place in which Christ put Himself, He shut off those theories of the Atonement that wear the priestly cast. But, in spite of His own definition of His work, it was early transferred to the other camp and became priestly in form and spirit. Christ is made an oblation and His blood atones. This interpretation puts Him where He refused to stand. An altar is put in place of the cross He endured and laid on every man's shoulder, and blood is made to do the work of obedience. The prophetic element fell into abeyance, and the priestly came to the front, so hard was it to rid the mind of magical conceptions of religion and to realise the force of moral laws.

Nothing is plainer than that Christ—starting in the prophetic—established another order than the priestly, into which He put Himself, His teaching, His conduct, His life, and His death—namely, the order of Fatherhood and Sonship with its corollary of Brotherhood. It was the order of universal human life. He knew nothing of a fall, or a curse, or of federal headship, or of decrees of election and reprobation. He recognised only that He was the Son of the Father, and that He was in the world to turn that relation into a Gospel of good news and salvation. The Fatherhood of God dominated all in Christ, and embraced all in Him and in His work. Whatever cannot be found in Fatherhood cannot be found in Christ, nor in anything done by Him, or that proceeds from Him. Absolute Fatherhood and absolute Sonship, this is the good news of the Gospel; it is the religion of humanity; it makes Christianity universal and eternal. Fatherhood and Sonship always have been and always will be; they are everywhere; in all ages and all nations; they create society, make laws, establish customs; they form the all-embracing law or fact of the world, and probably of the universe. It is here that the Atonement has full expression. Whatever it is and does, it simply carries out the relation of Father and Son. Nothing alien in spirit or idea must enter into it. No mysterious neces-

sity, no governmental exigency, no expiation of
guilt or propitiation of wrath, or satisfaction
of justice can be found in it, unless found in
the heart of fatherhood and in the relation of
father and son. Everything is simple, natural,
universal. A son obeys; if he disobeys he
incurs suffering and misery in body and spirit;
if he repents he is forgiven and restored.
Christ thus put the process of recovery from
sin into the parable of the lost son. To omit
from it the very thing that constitutes it is to
trifle with it as a teaching. To supplement it
by making *addenda* of expiatory sacrifice or
governmental necessity is to remind Christ
that He forgot to include them. The prodigal
has come back to the Father's house, humble
and penitent, and is forgiven out of the fulness
of paternal love, in order that he may once
more enter into sonship. This parable was
Christ's supreme teaching upon the restoration
of lost relations between father and son, *i.e.*,
between God and man. It involves repentance,
forgiveness, acceptance, justification, sancti-
fication, and other things that enter into salva-

tion; for to be a father and to be a son is to stand in complex relations, but whatever there is of these will be germane to the relation both in spirit and form; and they will be far removed from the dogmatic forms in which they have been clothed. Under our conception they are natural, universal, and self-explaining; under the other conception they are restricted by the legalism of a nation and an age, by a ritualism that is Hebraic, and by conceptions of guilt and desert drawn from data that no longer exist.

But Fatherhood and Sonship imply Brotherhood. Here are three cosmic facts—the ideal and the sole foundation of human society. The justification of Christ's divinity is that He gave His life even unto death to the full revelation and enforcement of this threefold relation. What was His method? Being a Son of the Father, His work is to bring all men into Sonship. Nothing can go beyond this, and He must not fall short of it. His task was to effect it. How? By drawing all men unto Him— not merely to be forgiven at the foot of His cross, but to undergo a far larger process (for man is something more than a sinner)—namely, to be made a partaker of His own life and death —one with Him in His obedience and sacrificial love. If He can make a man one with Himself, He has saved him from his sins and made him a son of God along with Himself. Thus the end of creation is served. God made man in His own image, and it is brought out by sonship. But this process is not complete nor in any degree efficacious, until Christ has brought the man to die unto his own sins and to give himself in self-sacrificing love to his fellow men. Thus the trilogy of Fatherhood, Sonship and Brotherhood is carried out; "as Thou, Father, art in Me, and I in Thee, that they also may be one in us." Now, this simple and natural, but stupendous process does not wear the cast of expiation, with its obvious suggestion that a debt being paid, or an impediment removed, man is somehow relieved of some danger, or from some obligation to pay a debt that Christ has paid, with the further suggestion of safety —a view that eliminates grace and forgiveness as unnecessary—and its accompanying snare of restful ease and inaction, with brotherhood left out except in some formal sense. The Atonement is not to be found in such a world as this. Instead, Christ takes us into a world that contradicts it. The subject of redemption is redeemed by himself becoming a redeemer, nor is he redeemed except as he *thus* enters into Christ's redeeming life.

If this confounds accepted theological distinctions, so be it. Christ saved the world not by theology but by a *life*. It is not, however, untheological; nothing in theology has a sounder basis than that Christ saved the world by Himself becoming a redeemer; that is, by passing through those moral processes that in themselves constitute salvation. It follows as day the night that the process must be the same for every man. If, in the Epistles, the sacrifice of Christ runs off into Hebraic or mystical expression, it continually returns to the norm of sonship and obedience, for here only its law or nature can be found. It may be spread out so as to touch life at many points, but it is at heart the living obedience of the Son to the Father. It covers sin, but it covers as much more of life as there is more in life than sin. It is difficult to get out of the dogmatic circle, and harder still to escape the narrowing effect of words and phrases; hardest of all to put due meaning into the universal and eternal truths and forces that made up the life of Christ as the revelation of the Father. The Atonement of Christ is the reconcilement of humanity in all the length and breadth of its complex duties and experiences. Hence He summons every man to a fellowship with His own life—not only to follow Him, but to become one with Him. At no point and in no moment s He without humanity at His side, in fellowship with it, in order that it may pass through His experience with Him. Thus only is it that men become one with Him *as* He and the Father are one. Thus all are acting under one eternal and universal law of love, and are achieving the reconcilement of God and man. It is foreign to the whole matter of Christ's life and work to put into it anything that does

not normally belong to the life of every man.
To do this would be to exclude it, so far forth,
from the order of humanity, and to break up
the unity which He came to ratify. He
became the redeemer of the world by making
every man a redeemer. In His life and death
He draws all unto Himself where, one with
Him, they die unto evil and live unto righteousness. Every man must go into the wilderness
of temptation, and put himself into the sufferings and under the burdens of the common
humanity, and bear witness to the truth even
at the cost of all. Each has his cross—bearing which he follows the Master and so gains
salvation, because *it is in itself a saving process*.

It is in this region of thought that Bushnell
found his leading idea on the subject, and from
which he never departed, namely, "vicarious
sacrifice grounded in principles of universal
obligation," a phrase that resists all counter
argument. It leads into the very heart and to
the very end of the Atonement. Christ did not
die for certain specific ends, but in fulfilment
of His life in all the relations in which He

found Himself. "He is not here simply to die, but dies because He is here." He fills out the relations of Sonship, which can only be done by self-sacrifice in conflict with evil. Thus only can He reveal the Father, and when this is done, even unto death, He has disclosed the reality, of the all-comprehending relation— what it is, what it requires, and what it will do. It is thus that men become true sons of God, by a faith in Christ that makes them one with Him.

Now this is a natural process. It wears the cast of universality. Wherever there are fathers, and sons, and disobedience, and suffering love, and repentance, and returning obedience, the work of Christ is unquestioned. Its very simplicity is a hindrance to its reception, but the duty of the preacher is to show how great simple things are, and to teach men that the highest problems of life and destiny are solved in the relations in which they find themselves as human beings. Life is explained by life itself.

Let us not be tempted to think that the redemption of the world is something apart from the eternal laws bedded in humanity, or that what is for all nations, and all ages, and all grades of men is limited by judicial notions that wear the cast of some nation or age, or that it is a fulfilment of Hebrew ritual.

This series of papers will add something to clearing the doctrine of its localism and provincialism and superstition, but it will not be wholly clear until it undergoes the criticism of cultivated and devout minds in all nations. The world will not accept the Atonement until it has received a world-wide interpretation; and for that it must go to the play of human nature in its main relations.

Whatever Christ said upon the subject bears the mark of this universality. Everything is natural, and in the natural order. He uttered no word to show that between love and forgiveness there is some hindrance to pardon. Christ dies not to create grace, but to reveal it. He lives to make manifest, to bear witness and obey, and dies because He obeys. Such is the order of true and eternal life. It is all love and the obedience of love. Its saving power consists in the absoluteness of the revelation; it is God's love in human life.

St. Paul uses expiatory phrases, but it is an uncertain exegesis which claims that these carry his meaning. That is found in the trend of his thought and in those passages where in one way and another he indicates that Christ dies for men that they themselves may die unto sin and live unto righteousness; his root idea is not vicariousness with a view to bearing a penalty, but to securing fellowship of life.

This view of the Atonement is discredited in several ways—some of which will be noticed in closing.

1. It is said that it has but slight, if any, historical recognition; and that it lacks something that has always been regarded as essential. As to the first point, it is admitted that it has no full dogmatic recognition, but it has had a better recognition in the experience of saints in all ages. The dogmatic utterances

conflict—one drives out another; but the experience that makes believers true followers of Christ does not change, nor does it awaken dispute. As to the second point, the something that is regarded as essential is the very thing that varies from age to age. In one age it is a ransom from the claims of Satan; in another it is expiation of original sin, subdivided into numberless distinctions, and each held as essential; in another the governmental theory prevails, and Christ dies to maintain the moral government of God by honouring the law. But if the Anselmic and the Grotian theory each denies the central meaning of the other, what is their historical value? All theories and all thought maintain the vicariousness, for life itself is based on and consists in it. But what thought to-day binds itself by historic precedent? None but that of the Church; and there it is the source of its chief troubles; the dead past and the living present cannot agree. There are great Churches whose inheritance of dogma and ritual hang like millstones about their necks.

2. It is discredited because it is claimed to shut out the mystery of the Cross and its possible meanings. It is enough to say in answer that the Cross of Christ is the reverse of a mystery, because it is a revelation; it makes all things clear and luminous, and sets them in an order that is visible, and is no more a mystery than the family and human love. Not until it is obscured by making Christ an expiating victim or a factor in a governmental system does it become a mystery. Then, indeed, does it lapse into obscurity and furnish occasion for all sorts of conjecture, and become a mystery that deprives it of its full meaning and power. Christ Himself makes no mystery of His life or works or death beyond what is contained in the universal truth that to lose the life in love is to save it.

3. But the chief reason why it is discredited is that the immense significance of the facts that make it up—few and simple as they are— is not yet fully apprehended; and the reason for this is that the doctrine has been involved in such complexity — metaphysical, forensic,

exegetical—that it is not easy to think of
it as a plain and natural thing, as clear and
simple as love. It may be said, is this all?
Do you say that the natural outplay of God's
love as manifest in the life of His Son constitutes that great saving work known as
the Atonement? Yes, but we also say that
these facts—the Fatherhood of God, the Sonship of Christ, the Brotherhood of man—are
not yet realised in the immensity of their
meaning as containing in themselves the whole
life and work and destiny of man in the world.
Their power to change and uplift and redeem
and save is still unrealised. They have a
nominal place in the creeds and the rituals, but
no Church and no theology have yet given
them their due place as factors in the redemption of the world. Both hold a vague theory
that this is their function; but they are not so
defined and used as to do the saving work of
the Church. They are hung up as signs and
wrought into symbols and turned into a tri-
logistic phrase, but in a feeble degree only are
they changed into reality and made the measure

of faith and the rule of conduct. Christ did make them a reality and the law of life, and so saves the world.

When, passing by the dogmatic theories of the Atonement, the Church fixes its eye upon Christ as He fulfills these human relations in life, and in death as included in life, it will know how He saves the world, because it sees the very process in operation. Signs of this are seen in the change of emphasis, now going on, from the Atonement to the Incarnation. By the Incarnation is not meant anything of an ontological nature, but simply the oneness of God and humanity. This is the central truth of Christianity and the source of its doctrines and duties. It carries us into the life of Christ where—in its ongoing—we see the way in which man comes into his oneness with God. Thus the Atonement is merged into the Incarnation as the more comprehensive factor.

The mark of this transition of thought is its universality. In this respect it is putting itself into accord with the world's thought, which is like the cloud that moveth altogether if it move at all. The world is fast becoming one, and thought widens to comprehend it. Provincialism has had its day. Human nature, with its eternal laws, is coming to the front. Under its language the Babel of conflicting and local creeds is passing away, and men can speak in the common language of their hearts and passions. The problem before the Church in the opening century is the problem of missions. It is the logic of the unfolding world. But Christianity will not evangelise the nations on the strength of an inspired Bible and a doctrine of the Atonement struck through with Hebrew ritualism, and construed by mediæval logic from facts that have turned out to be composite legends. But Father, Son, and Holy Spirit; Love, Forgiveness, Righteousness— these in their simple and direct form are at home the world over, and are full of God's power because He hath made of one blood all nations of men, and is the Father of all.

www.ingramcontent.com/pod-product-compliance
Lightning Source LLC
Chambersburg PA
CBHW072131220426
43664CB00013B/2206